THE NEGROES SEND THEIR LOVE

Also by Sean Hill

Dangerous Goods
Blood Ties & Brown Liquor

THE NEGROES SEND THEIR LOVE

Poems,
Perspectives,
and
Possible Futures

SEAN HILL

MILKWEED EDITIONS

milkweed.org

Published 2026 by Milkweed Editions
Printed in Canada
Cover design by Mary Austin Speaker
Author photo by Brian Powers
26 27 28 29 30 5 4 3 2 1
First Edition

Library of Congress Cataloging-in-Publication Data

Names: Hill, Sean, 1976- author
Title: The negroes send their love : poems, perspectives, and possible futures / Sean Hill.
Description: First edition. | Minneapolis : Milkweed Editions, 2026. | Summary: "From antebellum Georgia to twenty-first century Alaska, from the Wild West to the Asteroid Belt in the twenty-fifth century, this collection excavates the complexity of heritage and privilege, fatherhood amid environmental collapse, and the inherited memories, abilities, hardships, and love that link Black people living centuries apart"-- Provided by publisher.
Identifiers: LCCN 2025036581 (print) | LCCN 2025036582 (ebook) | ISBN 9781639550364 trade paperback | ISBN 9781639550371 ebook
Subjects: LCSH: African Americans--Poetry | African Americans--Fiction | LCGFT: Poetry | Essays
Classification: LCC PS3608.I43775 N44 2026 (print) | LCC PS3608.I43775 (ebook)
LC record available at https://lccn.loc.gov/2025036581
LC ebook record available at https://lccn.loc.gov/2025036582

for

my mother & brother, my father, wife & son,
my aunties & uncle, all the cousins,
and all the Negroes I love

Contents

Tests of Lessons Learned 1

MANSION SUITE

Necessarily a Negro 7
Mansion Couplets 10
Governor's Mansion Hands 11
Jim the Steward 13
Mansions Ars Poetica, 1863 15
The Hand in Which 17
Laws of the Land 18
Handy in Horse-Trading 19
A Negro Cook's Recipe for Home in the Slaveholding South 20
Where I Live 21
It Don't Shine Directly on My Gun 22
In the Kitchen with Celia 23
Parole, 1865 29
The Lake Sturgeon of Southern Appalachia 40

A WORLD TOGETHER

Where I Live [Redux] 45
Clarissa Lands, 1865 49
The White-Headed Woodpecker 51
Pearl & Lee, 1907 53

Mary Turner's Child's Peace Unborn 54
Life, Yet: A Family Story 58
March Photo Essay—Milledgeville, 1972 74
Before They Could Tell Him Where to Go 80
The Honey Drawl 82
The Pull That's Sung 83
The State: An Orderly's Remembrance, 2005 84
The Cicadas' Drone ~ Draws Me When Away 86
Homes in the House of the Sun 87

BEFORE & AFTER

Denali, 2012 91
Fairbanks, Alaska, Late August 93
Fairbanks, Alaska, Early September 94
Musica Universalis: A Nocturne 96
Postcard from Compass Rose 98
Goodnight 99
The Sight of Birds 100
An Autumn Aubade 102
Hello 103
What Was North 105
Life, Yet: In Carmel 109
In the Beginning 114
What Luck 115
Almost Solstice Serenade 116
One Saturday Morning in Carmel 118

NOTHING BUT POTENTIAL

Dangerous Goods [Redux] 131
Bodies & Selves 135
To Be Born in the Briar Patch 137
About Danger 144

ANCESTORS DREAMING

What You Studyin' On: An Environmental Statement 147
The American Pika 154
A Father and Son Speak About Internal Combustion 156
A Father and Son Speak About the Painting *A Desperate Stand* by Charles M. Russell 157
A Father and Son Speak About Perspective 160
A Father and Son Speak About Distinctions 162
Dear Alyce, 163
The Western Tanager *or* Why Montana 164
Every Different Day the Same: A Pandemic Memoir from Montana 166
Give Me a Small Ocean 168
The Lingering 171
Sounding a Silhouette 173
A Father Speaks to His Son About Reckless Behavior 175
After the Apocalypse *or* Notes on, Perhaps, the Future 176
Imagine We're Ancestors Dreaming 178

IN THE HOUSE OF THE SUN

A Negro Speaks of Worlds 183

★

A Negro Speaks on Community Relations in the Twenty-Third Century 190
from the script of the 2156 documentary *Hammer & Drill: On Exacting a Living in the Belt* 192
What You Want to Know 198
Complected Boundaries, 2338 199
A Negro Speaks of Lewis Temple in 2293 201
The Negroes Send Their Love 202

AN EPILOGUE

The Negroes Send Their Love 205

Notes on the Work 209
Acknowledgments 211

Always a knit of identity, always distinction,
always a breed of life.

—**WALT WHITMAN**

"Song of Myself"

come into the
black
and live

—**LUCILLE CLIFTON**

"after kent state"

There's nothing new
under the sun,
but there are new suns.

—**OCTAVIA BUTLER**

Parable of the Trickster,
an unpublished novel

THE NEGROES SEND THEIR LOVE

Tests of Lessons Learned

"Who was that white boy you was talking to?" asked G. We were standing in one of the wide spaces of the Hatcher Square Mall in Milledgeville, Georgia, the town where we were born and raised. Milledgeville is small, about 18,000 people in town and 22,000 folks in the surrounding county. My friend G lived in the county, what we referred to as "the country." It was 1989 or '90, and we were in high school. I was enjoying the freedom afforded me at that age. I had a 1978 Monte Carlo (a sun-bleached blue hooptie) and a late curfew, which meant hours to spend how I saw fit. But this isn't about high school adventures. This is about the boy I was talking to who was walking away as G approached—the white boy—and about the question itself. The "white boy" in question was my cousin. He wasn't white then and isn't white now. Neither *were* nor *are* either of his parents white. He was a Black boy who's now a Black man. And as I've said, he's family. A few years younger than me, I've known him all his life. He's certainly fair—light-skinned—and had loose curly hair—what folks might have called "that real good hair." But he wasn't and isn't white.

I laughed at the question, and said, "That wasn't no white boy; that was my cousin." I could understand the confusion from some distance, but surely if G had seen him up close, he wouldn't have asked that question. We'd been raised in a place where the range of expressions of Black bodily forms America birthed over the centuries was us—family, friends, and community that ranged from skin so light as to be why-not-white to skin dark as you can imagine and noses wide as Africa or aquiline narrow, not to mention the range of lips and hips and everything else—was people. Society had taught us about whiteness and the demarcating color line, had taught us how to understand race and Other, what was alien. And family had taught me how to see family. Had he gotten closer, G may have even recognized my cousin from the community.

Some weeks or months after that episode, as I walked out to my car to head to school, I saw my father out by the road talking to someone, a woman, a white woman, who'd stopped her car in front of our driveway. His body language and what I could see of hers made it clear that they knew each other, and she wasn't somebody who'd gotten lost in our neighborhood or something. Watching my father and this white woman felt strange. For all the life I've known him, my father has been an outgoing garrulous guy—he's rarely met a stranger. His comportment said this white woman was a close friend, perhaps a classmate. But my father had grown up in the Jim Crow South and graduated from a legally segregated high school and attended an HBCU, and so had no white classmates. That's when I realized over the course of our lives together, I'd come to understand the subtle differences between the registers of my father's gregariousness with white people and Black people, which made what I witnessed unsettling. He wasn't being the him he was with white people. They shared a laugh—one that rocked my father's body—and the woman drove off as I approached. Curious, I asked my father who that woman was. It was my light-skinned cousin's mom—one of those cousins of my dad's generation that I think of as an aunt. She was showing off her new car. I didn't recognize her as family or even as another Black person because she was driving an unfamiliar car.

My understanding of race and that color line shifted then, a little. I mean, I began to have an inkling, a sense of them as similar to the lines drawn as borders on political maps that occasionally follow rivers or mountain ranges, or trace the edge of some expanse denoting physical differences in the world, but are mostly imagined lines asserting agendas of power.

MANSION SUITE

Milledgeville is on Georgia's Antebellum Trail, a tourists' route from Athens to Milledgeville to Macon. The trail goes through the towns of Watkinsville, Madison, Eatonton, and Old Clinton. House Resolution No. 52, passed in 1985 designating the trail, states: "the gracious and leisurely wonder of [the antebellum] period elicit fond and soothing memories in these modern and hectic times; and . . . in remembrance of this historic and charming period, it is only fitting and proper to designate a portion of this highway as the Antebellum Trail."

So, Milledgeville touts itself as the Antebellum Capital, and it was that. But it was also, for the duration of the Civil War, the Confederate Capital of Georgia. It was where Joseph Emerson Brown, the governor of Georgia from November 6, 1857, till June 17, 1865, lived with his family in the Governor's Mansion. At that time governors brought enslaved folks, people they held as property, from their plantations to work as the household staff at the Governor's Mansion. I wonder whether the drafters of the Antebellum Trail resolution had in mind that the enslavement, the *involuntary servitude*, of those negroes was built into the creation of those supposed "fond and soothing memories."

I remember getting my first tour of the Old Governor's Mansion in third or fourth grade. My classmates and I, this group of Black and white kids, were told by the tour guide that the bricks used to build the mansion were made by enslaved people before she went on to tell us about all the great men who'd lived there as governor. This would have been in the early

1980s, and I think we had some little sense of the people the tour guide was referring to as "slaves." Twenty-odd years later, I would get my second tour.

My father, proud that his son had written and was getting published "a book about Milledgeville," told anyone who would listen that the book would be published soon, including his insurance man, a white father proud that his white son, Matt Davis, was the Assistant Curator of Education at the Old Governor's Mansion. They thought he should give me a tour of the mansion, and I was curious about what the visit would be like those many years later. That's how in 2007 I got my second tour.

Davis and his colleagues were developing a tour that focused on the Black folk who lived and worked at the mansion. I could scarcely have imagined this kind of visit only a few years earlier, so I felt lucky to get it then. It piqued my interest in the Browns and their household, in particular.

I went to the archives to read some letters written by Gov. Brown and his wife, Elizabeth Grisham Brown. I wanted to get a sense of them, and since there was a record, I could. In a letter dated November 29, 1858, Mrs. Brown writes home to her mother and sister at their plantation about the "big levee" they had at the Governor's Mansion right before Thanksgiving—all the preparations, the food, the people, the festivities. This letter struck me because caught between its closing sentences, *Hoping you are all well, we will expect to hear from you shortly. Mr. Brown and the children join me in love to you all*, and her signing, *Yours most affectionately, E. Brown*, she writes, *The negroes send love to their friends*.

Those words in that letter struck me when I first read them in typescript in part because *negroes* seemed in some way polite when other words, derogatory words, one in particular could have been used. But *negroes*, *colored*, *black*, or any number of words Mrs. Brown could have used to draw lines of race in that letter would not have changed those folks' legal status as property. And I was struck that she would think to include their sentiment and ask that it be passed along to their "friends." This speaks to a kind of intimacy.

Almost ten years later, I was finally able to get back to the archives and was able to read the original letter written in her hand, a lovely casual cursive that goes from one edge of the page to the other. I got to touch it with my hand. I got to verify that she'd written what I'd read in the typescript: *The negroes send love to their friends*. I'd thought about the letter for near a decade.

Those words had stuck with me because there is so much there that speaks to the situation those Black folk were in then and the situation Black folk are in now. That is being caught up in someone else's agenda, no matter whether the intent is malicious or benign, or they're simply indifferent to the effects their understanding of *them* and *us* has on Black folk.

Mansion Couplets

Spring, and negroes breathe the waft
of blossoms sweet on the morning breeze.

Dawn is the rooster's crow moving
feet to stride to where hands need to be.

The sweeping broom's insistent shoo,
woodsmoke, and today's baking bread.

Sloshing milk in the churn, a negro works the dasher;
A negro empties chamber pots of the night's water and dirt.

Governor's Mansion Hands

—Milledgeville, Georgia, 1858

The hand in which the laws of the land
were penned was that of a white man.

Hand, servant, same as bondsman, slave,
and necessarily a negro in this context,
but not all blacks were held in bondage
though bound by the constructed fetters
of race—in this case an expedient
economic tool for making a class of
women and men kept in place based
on the color writ across their faces—
a conservative notion for keeping power
in the hands of the few. It kept the threat
held over the heads of all negroes,
including those free blacks, who after
the coming war would be called
the formerly free people of color
once we were all ostensibly free.

Hands, enslaved, handled clay
and molds in the making of bricks
to build this big house for the gathering
of those few men with their white faces
who hold power like the end of the rope.

Hand, what's needed to wed, and a ring
or broom. Hand, a horse measure, handy

in horse-trading. We also call the pointers
on the clock that go around marking time
in this occidental fashion, handy for business
transactions, hands.

Jim the Steward

In a mansion is where I live. Greek Revival style they call it, but maybe that don't tell you much. It's got big columns on the front. My room's in the southeast corner—the side the sun rise on. I got a window with glass panes that look out on the garden. It's the most comfortable room I spec a negro could ever have. I'm what Master Brown call a steward. Ain't much on my walls—not like the rest of the mansion. They's thick plaster-covered brick walls. The house go up two more floors—what they call flights or stories. Negroes made all those bricks. My ceiling Master Brown's floors. Mine's the onliest room that's a body's on this level. Celia the cook, and she live in the cabin in back, and that's where York the driver stay too. Celia's daughter Emma the nursemaid. Emma sleep upstairs along with the Master and Missus, so she can care for the Brown chillun. My room got a rug. It's a leftover piece from the carpet in the rest of the house. As steward, I helps with the running of the house. Missus Brown's in charge of the household, but I'm right under her. I got the keys. Part of my charge is to protect the silver and china kept on this floor. I watch who come and go in and out of the house. On my windowsill ain't much special—no keepsakes. And no whiskey bottle either, for certain; Master Brown don't allow that in his house. And, if I had any, I wouldn't leave my free papers on the windowsill. There's light on the sill, but it don't shine directly on my gun. I'm one of the few negroes got a gun. I uses it to hunt up food for the house sometimes. Master Brown likes game. He like it better than some of this fancy food Celia have to make for the big dinners for the important people what come here. Fore we left Missus Brown's people's place, I ain't seen much beyond right round there. Now we here in Milledgeville, and I can't see my kin back on the farm. Master Brown over Georgia; he run the state, and that's why we live in this big house. I makes sure the doors locked and the house safe before I go to bed each night.

Mansions Ars Poetica, 1863

In an old story, the Almighty shaped clay
with His hands to fashion the first man.
In this story, enslaved hands shaped clay

to make bricks to build storied big houses
that will stand in this land. Both stories
lead on to sagas of births—natal tales

filled with first wails and nations of folk
and feats of nation-building. Birthing
a nation is building a narrative. In this tale

of rebellion and in future yarns of revolts
and insurrections, characters spout off
about representation and states' rights,

slavery and freedom, overreach and
gradualism. In these stories, framing
and pacing are key to creating suspense

with all deliberate speed. In birth
a footling's a breech baby trying
to stride right into the work of life.

A foot soldier's breech-loading rifle
is one tool being used for the work
of driving agendas and building identity

in this current convulsive revolt of the nation's
sense of self. In this epic of rebellion,
the casus belli are the negroes' bodies,

loves, and needful dignity. In smithing,
suppose forging metal for shoeing horses
sounds distinct from shaping metal

for spades or sabers or for shackles
and manacles, and know you can hold
the difference and build with that anew.

The Hand in Which

Hand as in handwriting, which
is awful in my case, so I type,
but way back when, by which
I mean up until only 150-odd years
ago or so—two long-lived lives—
few folks like me legally had a hand,
so, every last keystroke matters.

Laws of the Land

What's needed is a floating note on the laws
that constructed race in the old colonies
and young states, but that deserves
a library's worth of writing.

Handy in Horse-Trading

Was a time prospective buyers
would inspect negroes like horses
or cattle and look in their mouths.

Was a time after the buying and selling
when in some parts trouble would follow
a Negro for looking a white man in the eyes.

Notions held of Negroes now still redound
to beatings and

A Negro Cook's Recipe for Home in the Slaveholding South

INGREDIENTS—

1 negro's body and brains
3/5 fresh sorrowfuls of nostalgia / for what was your own / or your ancestors' home / from their recollections and remembrances
1 scant delightful of nights spent well with what's left at the end of day of a lover soon to be well spent
1 light joyful of laughter with family born-to or brought together
1/2 mindful of lives to come—yet to be born
1 pinch of pride of place (optional)

MODE—Mix in a beating receptacle about the size of your clenched fist. Braise in vessel with what liquid you have on hand; muscadine wine works well as does bone stock.

TIME—a blink, a span, or a lifetime

NOTE—Season to taste. Variations: Some ingredients and ratios change in the late nineteenth, twentieth, twenty-first, and even twenty-fifth centuries, but the end results are still Home.

20

Where I Live

You know, sometimes I remember the "I" always lives in a context—spatial and temporal. I think that is a generous place to start.

You know, I sometimes am obsessed with the times. | How did we get here? (It involved a when and most likely a wind—prevailing perhaps.) | And how's the view? |

You know, I love how the "I" in Langston Hughes's poem "The Negro Speaks of Rivers" becomes this beautiful communal being thanks to that definite article in the title. This is not *a* long-lived Negro who's been around since "dawns were young" and has known the human lives intertwined with the multifaceted lives of "ancient, dusky rivers." This Negro is "*the* Negro"—we, plural in the singular, a collective, a communal "I," the way a blues singer might could speak to and through and for an audience with the story of their "I"—an "I" so capacious and generous.

And you know, here there's an "I" that is a putting on of the mask that engages the persona like the vessel of the multitudinous "I"s we hold in our whole bodies, an "I" that is encompassing and tries to consider all the Negroes before me and in this collection and after me, the poet.

It Don't Shine Directly on My Gun

What's needed is a floating note on Nat Turner's Rebellion
and Denmark Vesey and the tightening of the slave codes
every time organized negroes challenged whites' tight grip

Negroes planning and making moves

How about getting Nat Turner and Denmark Vesey to the spades
table and David Walker can be Toussaint's partner and
Jemmy and Gabriel have a hard time waiting to get dealt a hand

Meditations on how to get some guns before . . .

When I spent nights at my auntie's house, there would be
a pistol under her pillow, just in case—closer at hand
than the nightstand where Nana kept hers

In the Kitchen with Celia

The kitchen her domain, a hot continent
of her own, as much as can be as long as
she keeps the house, the Browns, well-fed.

———

kettle
hooks for hanging things

rod
dutch oven
canisters
          table

sifter, mixing bowls, and measuring spoons & cups,
whisk

knives, forks, spoons, the dinner service
warming box

          patterned oilcloth
cutting board
                    flyswatter, dustpan, and broom

ash bucket and shovel next to the wood

fireplace
spit in the fireplace

dumbwaiter to serve the rest of the house

butter churn with dasher for the clabber

grinder

larder

———

Some kitchen objects have handles worn smooth by hands, an incidental rubbing with sweat and oils, and pots and pans carry seasoning (contain processes and eventualities—kitchen memories) and their heft has weight, can transport us with our touch or a taste of the food from them. Objects bear witness to kitchen witnesses—cooks.

———

I wonder what Celia makes of that man
from Macon come here to bake when
company, what they call a State gathering,
demands. They love his specialty, Apples à la
Parisienne. I wonder what Celia makes of that
Mister Freeman, that negro and his freedom.

I wonder if Celia sees herself as governor-fueler,
greasing the machine, though her food nourishes
this politician up to and through what they'll
call a rebellion to keep to their ways, including
foremost the holding of Celia and vast hosts of
negroes and their generations to come in bondage.

I wonder what Celia thinks about the fact
that Governor Brown would rather have her
cook shad pulled fresh from the Oconee at
the end of Jim's cane pole or something Jim
shot in the woods around with his flintlock than
any of the fancy dishes she makes for their levees.
I wonder what she prefers to cook and what dish
her dear Emma most desires from this kitchen.

———

I see Celia in line with countless other Black cooks; some we know like Hercules Posey, held by Washington—sent back and forth from Mount Vernon to Philadelphia—from slave-holding state to free and back again to keep him according to the laws and to keep him cooking and Jefferson's chef, James, James Hemings, Sally's brother, whom TJ took to France to be trained. James, he brought back macaroni and cheese for the president and now it's for the people. James had to train his brother to take his place before he could leave the place, Monticello. Zephyr Wright was LBJ's cook at the White House, and before that he was a representative; she had his ear and told it like it was for her and hers. And before that and after the war Malinda Russell published *A Domestic Cook Book: Containing a Careful Selection of Useful Receipts for the Kitchen* in 1866, the first cookbook known to be written by a Negro woman. In 1881, Abby Fisher, another Negro woman, published the Black-woman-authored cookbook, *What Mrs. Fisher Knows About Old Southern Cooking, Soups, Pickles, Preserves, Etc.* This is what we know and what we got receipts for. Negroes learned to cook where they did. Most in the quarters, many in the plantation kitchens, in the mansion, some at home, some in college, a few in France now—many putting they foot in it like my grandma and aunties, reminding us to put okra in the stew if you know what's good for you. Cooks—the hands and hearts that make the food—tell of journeys, hold our heritage, and bear witness. I'm grateful for what receipts we got and for what we know.

———

A negro cook's recipe for
Freedom in the Slaveholding
South calls for 1 very first
breath and 1 pinch of the
independence we've all
at one moment felt and a 1/2
mindful of the ancestors'
struggles and 1 heavy needful
of respect for the negroes'
bodies & loves and 1/2 a playful
of leavening care and 1 runaway
returned (you, a loved one,
someone new to the place,
or a story told of one whose
decisions and actions open
a space to consider questions
of home) and 1 last breath
(preferably not your own)
and 1 heaping joyful of
the ability to go see your
people and not have to rely
on the person who claims
to own you to relate your love
to your friends and kin (this
last is optional). Season to taste.

Parole, 1865

On a day in early May, the governor, the man
who ran Georgia during the recently ended Civil
War, signed a promise, a pledge, a parole—made
his word his bond; gave his oath, for what it's worth.

———

Our word *parole* comes from the French for "word." And in this context, one gives one's word—their "parole"—in order to rejoin the fold of society, stepping out of one way of being seen into another on a promise.

Head Quarters Cavalry Corps M.D.M.
Macon, Ga. May 8th, 1865.

I, Joseph E. Brown, Commander in Chief of the Militia of Georgia and State troops, do solemnly agree and pledge my honor that I will not bear arms against the United States of America, or give any information, or do any military duty whatever against said United States, and further that I will not as Commander in Chief or otherwise permit so far as it is in my power to prevent it and will not counsel any other officers or men under my Command to do any act of hostility to the United States or inimical to a permanent peace upon the basis of the Union under the Constitution and laws of the United States until regularly relieved by the United States of this obligation by exchange or otherwise.

(Signed)
JOSEPH E. BROWN,
Commander in Chief of Militia & State troops.

———

Our word *promise* comes to us from the Latin *promissum* "something promised," from the past tense of the Latin verb *promittere* "to put forth, promise," from bringing together *pro-* "forward" and *mittere* "to send," that same "send" as in *manumit* "to send forth from the hand," to release another woman or man from slavery. It's our word for the assurance of a future to ourselves and others as in *I promise, word is bond*. *Promise* also means "potential" in some contexts as in *he shows great promise for* ________.

———

The oath the conceding Confederate governor signed was about the future. It was also about the past and what the governor and his confederates held to. It seeks to reconcile divergent perspectives, a difference of opinions on slavery, if not equality, the way most may call this recent war the Civil War and others the War Between the States or the War of Northern Aggression and some the War for Freedom, which is also an indication of what we cleave to. And after cleaving the nation in two, all these folks out on their words. What is a nation to do?

———

I Command the Militia
and troops and pledge
that I will bear arms against the United States of
America, give information
against said United States, and further that I will
Command other s so far as it is in
my power
to do any act
inimical to a permanent peace
under the Constitution and laws of the United
States until relieved by the United States of this obli-
gation .

(Signed)
,
Commander in Chief of Militia & troops.

inimical *to a permanent peace*—A funny word seldom heard, our adjective *inimical* comes to us from the Late Latin *inimicus*, from combining *in-* "not" and *amicus* "friend" and is related to the Old French *enemi* from which we get our word *enemy* by way of Middle English. We know the enemy, and that's important, crucial, swear 'fore God and all we love, to accept another's word to be not an enemy, if not a friend.

Folks in the future may know *amicus* from those court briefs occasionally mentioned in their news. Those “friend of the court” briefs, unverified stories couched as relevant and providing helpful context, are told solely to sway judges’ opinions and—

I

pledge

that I will bear the United States of America, give

said United States

my power to

do any act

under the Constitution and laws of the United States until relieved by the United States of this obligation .

(Signed)

,

.

On a day in early 2025, almost 160 years in the future, some folks won't need to step out on their word, be paroled. You see, on an early day in January 2021, after having cleaved to an oath—crossed their hearts behind a vote they'd cast that was counted in a democratic election that swung away from their desire—and holding to a narrative their savior spun and with their hearts burning (not crosses yet, nor crosshairs or iron sights yet) they acted out of their sense of entitlement in the name of their commander in chief and carried out a pledge to fight the peaceful transfer of power. After that, when back in power, he pardoned them for stepping up on his behalf, without even a pinkie swear to not commit *any act of hostility to the United States* again, I swear.

———

I

do

what

is in

my power to

to act

in peace

until relieved of this obli-

gation .

(Signed)

,

.

The Lake Sturgeon of Southern Appalachia

Acipenser fulvescens

When you think of fish, if you think of fish,
do you think of this fish? If so, do you think
of a dish of caviar or the Civil War?

For me these fish bring to mind
an elbow or knee, places we bend
where touch is close to the bone. Touch
your patella—from the Latin for a "small shallow dish,"
and this one upside down and covered, skin over bone plate—
you get close to the feel of sturgeon with their rows of scutes
(starting like *school* and ending like *boots*),
bony plates under their rough brown skin.

Since these drab late bloomers don't mate
till their teens or even twenties and then only
every three years or so, do you think *stodgy*
sturgeon? Did you know our appetites took
their generations before they could be?
Their roe fed an economy
for a time in the late nineteenth century.

Long-lived fish, these somber bottom-feeders
—the males live into our middle age;
the females can live to be one hundred and fifty or so
—twice our lifetimes.

If fish could talk, I would settle in with one of these
antique Tennesseans and ask
If fish had knees, when you were a fry
at your father's
how did he explain to you the cries
of men at the Battle of Chattanooga,
the thud of bodies come to rest, the boot-thump
of rough brogans, the report of rifle and cannon fire
—*Southern men* (not bending the knee to keep others
in their thrall, claiming generations before they could be,
using slave labor to feed the economy) *routed on the ridges*
above your home?
What rippled your sky?
Did you hear
cannon fire for thunderclap
and wait for rain?

That's what I would ask,
if fish could talk,
and I could find one
that survived the last century
in those Southern waters
we dammed and sullied.

A WORLD TOGETHER

Where I Live [Redux]

In his book *Milledgeville: Georgia's Antebellum Capital,* historian James C. Bonner states, "The emigration pattern of blacks was only a little different from that followed by whites, but there is little data on which to judge their success or failure in their new environment."

I understand this to mean there weren't any records kept of those Negroes' successes or failures, leastwise not the kind Bonner would turn to. This makes sense, since the recordkeeping all the selling and the buying of negroes required would have ceased after there was a surrender and a reconstruction and the settling of those amendments to the Constitution: the Thirteenth, Fourteenth, and Fifteenth, abolishing slavery, making negroes citizens, and guaranteeing them enfranchisement—the vote. Whereas before, they could tell us where to go, Negroes could legally move around more freely and choose where we live.

Bonner continues saying, "While a few moved to Northern states, most relocated in the more prosperous urban centers in Georgia. None are known to have settled west of the Mississippi, where they might have secured free homesteads on which to begin a new life. A few went to Liberia."

And as you know, some of us went north to what had been freedom, became upcountry cousins always seeking opportunity to meet their ambitions.

Though not necessarily from Milledgeville, a few of us made homes in the Middle West—Cleveland, Detroit, Chicago, and places like Gary, Milwaukee, and Des Moines, between the north & east and the farther west. And we can't forget those Negroes settling upriver in Minneapolis toward where the Mississippi starts to flow from the Northwoods. All created lives from the confluence of ambition and opportunity.

And some of us went to that farther west, reaching out of the South to land of open spaces, to other communities and frontiers—exploring and settling—in places like Kansas, Oklahoma, Colorado, and Montana and other territories in the West. The fact of this migration runs counter to the West of the Popular Imagination. Who was the Wild West? What did Bonner know?

And as Bonner said, some of us even went across the ocean to Liberia—this time Negroes boarded boats willingly for the promise of determining their destinies in their mothers' lands. Speaking to this sense of a Negro being free to reach one's potential in Liberia, Allen Yancy, an 1872 emigrant from neighboring Hancock County, GA, said, *I am satisfied that I can make my living here, and any other man can who has brains and can work*. And, not that it much matters, the Southern white folks wrote two different stories in the newspapers showing they didn't know whether to say good riddance to difficult Negroes or goodbye to good hands—the bottom line for them being some bodies needed to do those "Black jobs" round there.

I've set foot in all fifty of America's united states and five of Canada's provinces and one of its territories; over the years, I've expanded my range map like a bird species finding more habitable space at the edges of its range over time. But you know, wherever I've been I was sure I wasn't the first Black person to show up there. Of all the places outside of the South I've called home, I've known I wasn't the first of us to call it that either.

There is a stunning hummingbird native to Panama in the scientific collection of the Museum of the North in Fairbanks, Alaska. The Green-crowned brilliant (*Heliodoxa jacula*—"the sun's glory or magnificence" and "darting") is a little emerald-green bird with a sapphire-blue gorget that shines in the light like it's lit from the inside, like a twinkling green piece of the sun; its feathers seem to somehow reflect more light than surrounds it.

This bird specimen ended up in the museum's collection because some birds born and reared in the Alaskan summer spend their winters in Panama before returning to Alaska to rear young of their own, and the scientists wanted samples of the community that those birds are a part of throughout the year. A bird's political-border-ignoring migration across continents forms its own country—that bird's nation—which holds capacious communities.

And some of us moved to Southern cities not too far off. And some of us moved perhaps just a few miles off the place where they'd been held as property if they moved at all. And they lived in the freedom they fought for to grow in the South, the only home they'd known. They kept our culture and community in its natal home—the heart of our nation. They the cousins holding down the homeplace. And most all of us invited to the family reunion.

Clarissa Lands, 1865

Long ago, way before the story
involving you, water found the easy
way through this landscape, the only
way it knew—collected where gravity

guided, wended ever down, gathered
trickles to an eventual river, what
came to be called the Missouri,
and in the then war's waning you

traveled up that water by measures
to the territory of Montana, a land
of fresh starts. And one day in May,
perhaps feeling the first moments

of no longer being property of a man
and his wife (a woman who you look
so much like you could be her younger
duskier sister and probably are), you

disembark the *Lillie Martin* to freedom,
this after the Confederacy surrendered,
marking the end of a peculiar misery
for you and millions of your fellow

folk, the other end of a long journey
begun with so many embarkations
—the Middle Passage. So many
decisions brought you this far,

to this sublime land where you
step into the new light of freedom
(not even a teen) and have to lean
on the promise of Reconstruction

as the shadows of Black Codes and
Jim Crow grow like a river rising in
spring melt—old notions and new
abuses of those who look like you.

Yet in this heart-stretching land
you'll meet a young man, James,
and y'all will lay claim to a new
life and create a legacy.

The White-Headed Woodpecker

Quiet. Given to prying more than pecking, an odd member
of the family, lives only in the high pine forests of western

mountains like the Cascades, where I spent an afternoon
almost a decade ago in Roslyn, Washington, looking for what

I could find of Black people who'd migrated from the South
almost a century and a quarter prior. The white-headed

woodpecker doesn't migrate and so is found in its
home range year-round when it can be found. Roslyn,

founded as a coal mining town, drew miners from all over
Europe—as far away as Croatia—across the ocean, with

opportunities. With their hammering and drilling to extract
a living, woodpeckers could be considered arboreal miners.

A habitat, a home range, is where one can feed and house
oneself—meet the requirements of life—and propagate.

In 1888, those miners from many lands all in Roslyn came
together to go on strike against the mine management.

And so, from Southern states, a few hundred Black miners
were recruited with the promise of opportunities in Roslyn,

many with their families in tow, to break the strike. They
faced resentment and armed resistance, left in the dark

until their arrival, unwitting scabs—that healing that happens
after lacerations or abrasions. Things settled down as they do

sometimes, and eventually Blacks and whites entered a union
as equals. Black save for a white face and crown and a sliver

of white on its wings that flares to a crescent when they
spread for flight, the white-headed woodpecker is a study

in stark contrasts. Males have a patch of red feathers
on the back of their crowns, and I can't help but see blood.

Pearl & Lee, 1907

Pearl Payne and Lee Pleasant Driver,
two of the few Negroes in Anaconda,
Montana, a smelter town, found each other.
Lee, the protected side of something—
sheltered and sheltering—a pleasant
place out of the wind and rain. A pearl
grows from the need to soothe pain
—nacre encases irritants to smooth
rough edges and results in a luster
we appreciate, worthy of the necks
of our adored if we can afford it.
Smelting, extracting the metal from rock
or ore, copper in this case (valued because
it carries a current and connects people)
requires heat and care. Lee Pleasant,
a former buffalo soldier, saw worth
in Pearl Payne, and she in him. He, born
at the end of the war, and she, a dozen
years later, who didn't know slavery
but knew well what it meant to be
Black in a recently reconciled nation,
wed in that Western smelter town.

Mary Turner's Child's Peace Unborn

—May 19, 1918, near Valdosta, Georgia

It was to be Mary Turner's third child. It was made something else. It would never be a girl or boy, much less a woman or man. Its muscle, its wit, what grit it would have had, culled, killed in the name of a certain social order.

I was eight months grown
in my mama when she was
hanged or rather hung upside
down by her bound ankles
not like Styx-dipped Achilles.
Neither she nor I meant to be
nearly invulnerable, rather
our lot always assailable.

This is too much but is
our story. They doused
my mama with gasoline
and burned the clothes
from her body. They then
cut me from my mama—
not to be a Caesar like Julius,
but a harsh caesarean—
with a pig-splitting knife.

It's said I did take a couple
of breaths to cry before they
took a boot heel to my head
to expedite my death. I was
always meant to be the meat
of white supremacy. Its appetite
took me before I could be. What
failures I would have had were
not to be, were not mine to make,
as my successes were not to be had,
for they made their success final.

They lynched my papa
the day before for being
a Negro and having worked
for the killed white man
though he had no hand
in that rough man's death.

My mama spoke up, and—

My mama and papa's love pulled
me from the infinite, and the flame
of me quickened in my mama those
months before they drove the spirits
of us out of our husks like cicadas.

What the mob did and society didn't
do left so many hearts thereabouts
split just like a cicada's husk leaving
their spirits confirmed in the struggle.

———

They've worked hard to make me
one of so many of us folks taken
on boats, born into chattel slavery
in service of an economy, born in
service of an identity in the post-
Reconstruction reign of terror
to be caught up in convict leasing,
born into the urban redlining era,
born with policing and police killings
and the prison industrial fleecing
of our communities, of our people, and
in this nation built on our backs we're
expected to accept refineries, chemical
plants, and other such environmental
injustices in what backyards we make
for us.

"Gaw dammit," exhales Officer Murray, one of the two police officers standing in front of a small clapboard house and talking in the slant of light this morning in New Town, a close-knit colored community in Milledgeville. The tall, burly officer is white, of course, since Milledgeville won't get its first Black police officer till 1964, another dozen years hence. Murray isn't from this community, but he's known all over town for being rough with Negroes. Today is an accumulated day tacked on to the shortest month, a Leap Day, and it has already been an eventful morning.

"Yeah," agrees Officer Bolton, a stout man, before he adds, "What we gonna do about this black bastard?" They're talking about Augustus Herst, a young man who lives in the small house directly across the street from the Bakers, one of the two white families who lives there at the edge of New Town. Next to the Bakers' house is Mitchum's Store. The weathered hand-painted sign indicates as much, but since this store serves the New Town neighborhood the sign isn't necessary and so hasn't been repainted. In the early part of the next century, some who grew up in this community with this store will try to remember it with their middle-aged children who knew no such place when they were raised there. On the other side of the store, just off Jefferson Street, one of Milledgeville's thoroughfares, sat John Mitchum's house. Earlier that morning when Mr. Mitchum left his house, whistling as he always did on his way to open the store, he waved to Mrs. Carol Baker's older brother, Mr. Thomas Pritchard, who every so often came to stay with his sister's family. Mr.

Pritchard was on the porch feeding the cat. Almost as soon as he got in the store, Mr. Mitchum heard a gun report, small caliber, a .22 rifle—a squirrel gun. He thought nothing of it until he heard a woman scream. Mr. Mitchum went back out to investigate and found Mrs. Baker, kneeling over her brother Tom. "Tom's been shot," she shouted. "I think Gus shot Tom," and Mr. Mitchum turned on his heel and went back into his store to call the police from the only telephone in the neighborhood.

Now all Officer Murray can offer Officer Bolton is, "Damn crazy darkie."

And Officer Bolton asserts what's obvious to them both. "We gonna have to do something."

Neither of them wants to go into the house after Herst. They both stand silent for a moment before they notice an elderly woman approaching from down the road looking like she's going somewhere. Betty Cooper lives down past where the blacktop stops and the red clay road starts. She is older but not the oldest in her community and slight of frame but a big presence in the lives of her family and friends, while she's soft-spoken—quiet really—around white folks.

"Hey! Auntie," Officer Bolton says to get Betty's attention though they've held it since she first saw them as she walked up the hill. She'd hoped she wouldn't attract theirs, but that's not her luck today. She was just heading to Mitchum's for cornmeal for cornbread for this evening's supper.

"Yes, sir?" she answers, enunciating in a way to let the officer know he has her attention.

"There's this nigra fella in this house done shot and killed the man across the street," Officer Bolton informs Betty. He carries on saying, "Now, we want you to go in there and get him to come on out and talk to us. Can you do that? We need you to talk to him."

"Yessir," she replies, enunciating in a way to let the officer know he had command of her in that moment.

Betty's not sure what to do, how quickly to move around these men, so she takes a couple tentative steps that they may have mistakenly owed to her age, but before she gets too far, Officer Murray says, "If you can't get him to come out, you need to find out just how dangerous he is. You do that?"

"Yessir, can do that," answers Betty, a little unsure about her assurance.

Officer Murray draws his command to a point, saying, "He done already killed one white man today—one too many in any of y'all's lifetime."

The police officers move back across the street toward Mitchum's Store and the Baker home. Betty approaches the front door of the house the law officers had been standing in front of for the last little bit. Betty pauses at the door.

"Gus, it's Miss Betty from down the road. I'm coming in," she announces. With no response, Betty steps slowly across the threshold into the well-kept four-room shack. "Gus, you in here?" she asks because she doesn't know what else to say, and she carries on, "It's Miss Betty from down the road. Where you at? I just want to talk. Gus?" Betty hesitantly steps farther into the modest home. It's no cleaner but just a little nicer than her own shack in its layout and construction.

"You in here, Gus?" Betty asks again. There's nowhere to hide in this small living room and she can see no one's in the little kitchen. To fill the silence that followed her previous query, she asks, "Where you at?" Finally getting to why she's in this house, Betty says, "Them police out there want you.

They say you shot Mr. Tom." Still no response so she says, "Say you killed Mr. Tom. They want you."

Folks in the community knew Augustus was a touched young man, different from most folks, and might ought to be a patient at the state hospital. So, given what she's been told about Mr. Tom, Betty moves cautiously closer to what must be the first bedroom door. Moving slowly, Betty finds herself edging across the threshold asking, "Gus, you in here?"

In a whisper that sounds so loud in the silence that it startles Betty, Gus answers, "I'm in this closet, Miss Betty."

Betty trains her eyes on the closet on the other side of the bed. She waits a moment then tells that silence coming from the closet, "They wants to know how dangerous you is." And after three heartbeats, "You got that gun, Gus?"

Seven long heartbeats later, Gus asks, "They gon shoot me? They gon kill me, ain't they?"

"Yes, child, I imagine they aims to kill you," Betty breathes out this hard truth that she's known since well before this morning. Betty walks farther into the room to get closer to the closet and Gus.

"Ain't got no more bullets," Gus sighs. After a moment he asks, "You gon tell them I ain't got no bullets? So they can be brave enough to come shoot me?"

"I got to tell them something," says Betty.

"And, bullets or no bullets, either way this my end," says Gus. "It was so from the start." Then he asks, "Were you brave to come in here?"

"I ain't have much choice. They told me to come talk to you," says Betty, uttering a truth she couldn't see no way around before adding, "I guess, could be, brave and courage is in the *how* of your doing, not the *what*."

"What we doing is talking cross this threshold, me huddled up in this closet—a closet like the hanging side of a chifforobe, and I prolly won't live long enough to be hanged," Gus says, and sits quietly in that fact for a long moment. "And you done crossed the threshold into this house for them white men—them peck police. Life is just a series of crossings—passing out of or into one thing or another. We brung into this world from our mothers, take our first breath, and before we can walk, that breath right there—that one breath—is our first step toward the next big threshold, our last breath and death."

Betty can't let that kind of talk sit in the air for long. "We got God, though, child," she says. "You got God, ain't you? He in your heart?"

Considering Betty's questions for a blink, Gus answers, "They gon shoot that heart. They ain't gon arrest me, are they? You know how Murray is, and if he and Bolton arrest me, it'd be some other white men come down to the jail to get me. And they'd shoot me in the head, the heart, God knows where." Gus goes quiet for a few moments, considering where all they will shoot him, before he says, "They shot up them two couples up in Monroe something awful. Remember that?"

And as Gus says those words, the light seems to shift in the room Betty's standing in, and the sound of the space opens out and Gus's voice carries differently as the room and its closet seem to dissolve into and become a clearing in some woods. With the closet and its slight threshold gone, Betty sees Gus. The slender young man is hunkered down on the ground a few feet away. The rustle of brown thrashers and squirrels in the underbrush finds Betty's ears, and the sweet smell of spring that's bloomed into itself finds her nose.

Looking all around at what isn't a small bedroom anymore,

Betty, stunned, says, "Where we? How we get here? What you done?"

Gus stands slowly like a seed sprouting and says, "This happens to me sometimes. When the world that's been made around us is too much, I look inward, think about some other place or time, and what I find comes to me. I mean, moved by my feelings, sometimes my mind migrates and takes my body with it. It ain't got to be no time or place I been. Been that way since I was a boy." Taking a moment to look at the still stunned Betty, he says, "You the first to ever come with me though." Looking around the clearing, Gus says, "This must be where them folks was lynched." And indeed, the woods are those by the Apalachee River near Moore's Ford Bridge in Walton County where the lynching happened a few years ago one summer evening in late July. But it's quiet and cool in the shade this late spring day. It's probably sometime in May, and Betty is there with Gus. Neither of them has been to this place before; neither has been to Monroe much less Walton County even though it's only three counties over. Neither has ever had cause to go that far from Milledgeville, but they know this is after the mob of twenty white men stopped the car Roger Malcom, Dorothy Dorsey Malcom, George Dorsey, and Mae Murray Dorsey were in and after they bound the men and after they fired three volleys riddling the young couples with bullets and shot and after the investigation and after the bodies were removed by the morticians and after the white souvenir hunters and after further investigation and after no one was arrested, much less convicted, and after this place became the quiet place near the river again and settled into being a haunted place for the Black folk around here.

For a few long moments, they stand in this peaceful quiet,

different from the heavy hush of the house they'd been in. Gus says into the quiet, "And they say one of the women was seven months pregnant." And though that is what they said, it isn't necessarily a fact, but the truth of the matter is it sure could have been, given this nation's history of chattel slavery and the fact of the lynching of Black folk after the Civil War, after the occupying US troops were withdrawn to end Reconstruction. And especially given what they, that mob, that gathering of individuals, did to Mary Turner and her not-yet-child down in South Georgia thirty-odd years ago, that one of the women at Moore's Ford was pregnant can't be nothing but the truth. Since Gus and Betty's ancestors were brought to this land, the white terrorism they've faced and the threat of it has been steady. Again, into the quiet of this clearing Gus says, "I don't know why I done it."

Betty knows he means shooting Mr. Tom. She's a God-fearing Christian woman; she's been on this Earth sixty-four years using the five senses and the common sense He gave her, so though she might not condone violence, she knows why the oppressed might act against their oppressors. She says to Gus, "I've seen enough of the happenings on this world, and when I allow myself to know the way things is ain't the way they ought to be, I know why I'd take a notion to, God help me."

After sitting with Betty's acknowledgment of the ways Negro lives are circumscribed by white supremacy and conceding that might could be a motive to do what he done, Gus says, "I hear you, and I appreciate that, but it's my mind; it ain't right. And it's those couples that were murdered in this place six years ago and all of us since and all of us before. And maybe I was in my right mind in the moments when I aimed that gun at Mr. Tom instead of his cat or a squirrel or something, anything else, or just taking a breath and not squeezing that trigger. So many of us been killed. And for what? To keep them feeling over us? It's a bad situation." Betty listens and nods. And there is another quiet moment that Gus ends when he says, "How do we fix it? Can we repair this?"

"What you talking 'bout, baby? How to fix the situation you in?"

"Yessum, Miss Betty, this fix I'm in—this mess."

"Gus, child, I don't know."

"I guess I also mean the mess—the situation most all us Negroes in, leastwise the ones of us alive. And, to my way of thinking, being dead ain't no real solution. So how can this broke thing be repaired? What kind of reparations can be made to address this mess? Them Japanese gon get reparations from the nation, leastways some of them will."

Betty knows about the Second World War and about the Japanese and Pearl Harbor and all those people here who hadn't done nothing but be Americans until the government decided that wasn't enough and locked them away, but she don't know what Gus is talking about with reference to reparations. So, she stands quietly in this clearing and lets him talk.

He says, "You know, behind the treatment they got around the war—being forced out of what was theirs and being locked up. They started asking a few years ago. And *we* been pushing back and protesting and asking for repairs since they brung us here from across the water, leastwise some of us have, on the behalf of us all."

"Gus, baby, you talking out your head," says Betty. "I know this a lot on you, child, but you got to put some of it in God's hands. Hold what you can, and put the rest in God's hands, son," she says, using that word as any elder in this community might address a young man. She speaks his deed into this clearing and the world beyond, "You shot Mr. Tom this morning, and he dead and gone now."

In response, Gus asks, "You ever think about being remembered? About what stories folks, your folks, gone tell about you?" He says, "I wonder what kinda family story I'm gon make. So far, the story is I ain't always clothed in my right mind, but I'm all right mostly. You think about the things your daughters tell they children and this world about you? You got daughters, ain't you?" And with this question, the expanse of the clearing, the woods around it, the river, and the fields beyond contract back to the room Betty walked into, February light slanting in through the window again. The smell of spring blossoms and the feel of outdoors on their skin, gone in this room Gus now uses to hide from the authorities.

"Yes, I do," says Betty, thinking about her four daughters. "Two live here in New Town; one off in Atlanta getting her education—gon be a school teacher. She the first in the family to go to college; I feel blessed to see that." Betty thinks about her husband who was an old man when they met—theirs his third family; he was born in 1856 as someone's property. Now he got a daughter who going to college. "I'm proud of all my children. And one of my daughters all the way across the nation living in Los Angeles, California. I can't rightly imagine that—California. Nor a city as big as they say. Or all that water—the ocean." A roar rises and falls in the room as the room wavers and fades and they find themselves standing on a stretch of sand between an ocean and a city, both bigger than anything Betty has ever seen.

Gus makes note of this visit, saying, "I wondered once, maybe these transports of feelings, these flights to other places and times, come from our ancestors somewhere back down the line, and I went to some quarters one night when one of the deep ancestors was telling a story. Was saying she wasn't there at Igbo Landing, wasn't at the water's edge when those folks waded out and kept walking toward where the Orimili seemed to whisper from that far shore and on to Igboland. And she'd heard about folk that put down the work they were made to do, found their wings, rose up, and went home. She said she understood those folk recognized their power to choose and change, and she knew it to be so." That's how Gus knows surely some of the ancestors experienced episodes in bondage, when under the weight of the oppression, they created such spaces perhaps of, or maybe for, their inner lives. Gus says, "Some of these transports seem like little more than a thought, and I've come to find that even the longer ones really last only about as long as a thought, a blink, for those who don't go on them. But they create space enough for a body to go on." Then he asks, "What you think your daughters gon tell about you?" And they're back in the room.

Betty wonders about this last visit, was that city really Los Angeles and the ocean really the Pacific; she wonders how close she was to her daughter and grandchildren, but she answers, "I imagine they'll say I worked hard in my garden and was able to keep them fed and held in my love. I guess they'll say I raised them right—raised them up to be good folk."

"You think about your grandchildren and great grands and their lives? You wonder what them generations yet to be born, the ones you don't and won't know, gon know of you? Can you imagine a great grandson writing a *book* with a story with *you* in it?"

"No, child, I can't imagine that. And I don't think much

about the children that ain't here yet. I'm an old woman. I think about those I got now and about my God. And about what good I got and can do in this world. I'm a church mother at New Hope down 'cross from the house. I'm helping to raise my grandson, the one whose mama gone to Atlanta to get her education. He sure is some of the good I got in this world. He my fishing buddy. We goes to the river as much as we can, cane poles in hand. That time is a joy." In that moment, the room shifts again, and they're in the shade of a tree on the bank of the Oconee River where Betty and her grandson often fish. She and Gus stand there and catch a few notes of a birdsong before the room comes back. Betty finishes her thought, "Naw, beyond good folk, I don't think much about who my girls' children gon be."

"Miss Betty, some folks say I'm crazy, and I might be, but mostly I like to think it's just that I see more than most. You know, like a prophet or something. They think I'm crazy 'cause they think I shot Mr. Tom for no reason. But I ain't crazy. I shot him because of how he saw me." Gus continues, "I mean, I wouldn't shoot you, Miss Betty, because we *us*. I mean, I am *I*, and you *you*, but we both *us*. Wouldn't shoot nobody else around here except maybe another one of these crackers. To them, we the border and the frontier beyond—considered unsettled land to be exploited, that's a way they see Other. That's the way it's been, but I've come to know that ain't the way it should be. You know, I see a future where none of nobody see anybody else as *them*. We gon all be *us*. I think that's when the shooting'll stop. That ain't crazy. Is it?"

"Gus, child, I don't know. I think that we all God's childrens. And I do know you gon have to leave that there closet before long. I got a feeling them men's patience gon wear thin soon."

"Remember, we ain't been gone long, and they ain't said nothing in a little," Gus says. "They giving me some peace, so I'm gon sit in it for a minute. Can we be here awhile?" Gus contemplates the quiet a moment created and says, "When I squeezed that trigger and there was the noise, well, after that there was this silence. There's often a quiet that follows violence. And this is where we sitting as long as the patience of them police lasts. I aims to enjoy it. Though I'm not sure *enjoy* is the right word. There's this word *savor*, but that might not be it either."

"Where the gun at now, Gus? Is it in there with you? You sure you ain't got anymore bullets?"

"The gun over 'cross the room. Naw, I ain't got no more bullets for it. I found this peace," says Gus. "And 'sides, ain't bullets or guns enough to make this standoff last much longer like the Alamo." The Constitution—the Fourteenth Amendment to it—made Gus's freed ancestors and hence him part of *We the people*, and the Constitution says he's got the right to a gun and due process, and he's done something—committed a crime punishable by law, but he barely stands a chance if arrested, much less if he makes it to trial. Gus starts again, "The rule of law don't apply to us. It's the rule of they will. And won't they will."

"You best be thinking about your savior, son," says Betty. "Gus, you asked after my daughters a bit ago. Well, you know today one of they birthday. I brought her into this world on Leap Day, so her birthday comes around less than the rest. She my second. The first came on a day we celebrated Christ's rising. The third came on Independence Day. And the last came on Christ's birthday. They days wasn't they own or were off a little." Betty pauses in thought before saying, "I guess all our days off a little bit, mostly not our own, and numbered from the start. When was you born, Gus?"

"I was born on October 6—nothing special about that day," Gus says. "I was born between the wars and just before the Depression. Ain't nobody had much of nothing, they say. But I was a baby and ain't know no different. And 'sides, I had all I needed and all I knew to want."

"That's the truth." Betty says, nodding. "That's right, ain't nobody had much and us colored folk had less, but we a community, and we come together to share and keep going. And if I'm eating, you eating, and we do what we can to look after each other's children. Yeah, need was shared when it was."

They both sit for a moment seeming to think about what Betty just said before Gus says, "I imagine the story the white folks gon tell about this gon be 'Local Man Killed When Shot by Berserk Negro.' I see this future right there in the *Union-Recorder* soon. Mr. Tom the 'man' and I'm the 'berserk Negro.'" Gus looks in the direction of the window, but he's really looking inward when he says, "I wonder how that story gon grow. What story Mr. Tom's family gon tell? Will it be another in they Negro stories that make right to them why they treat us so?"

"Gus, you might be worrying after the wrong thing, son," Betty says. "You don't think they gon do what they gon do? Yeah, the wrong thing."

"They got their story of the Negro, and they make our stories of Negro towns—Rosewood, Greenwood, Forsyth—communities burned down or bombed or simply taken over like they done the Indians. I mean even the civilized Cherokee, who tried to show how much they had or could have in common, came up with their own writing and started newspapers and such. Some of them even built big ol' plantations and kept some of us Negroes as property. But soon as what was theirs had more value than the whites was willing to let them sit on, they was removed—sent off 'cross the country, because the whites' might mean they always in the right, huh?"

Gus and Betty sit quietly for a span before Gus says, "This the story of Negroes in this land, and I'm wondering about the place of story in all our lives—Negroes, whites, Indians, Japanese, Russians, Italians, Germans, Jews, all."

"What you mean, child?"

"Whites got they sundown towns. When Negroes ever burn down a whole town of whites'? Ever run them off from they homes and take they lands? They get together and draw up housing covenants and red lines on maps to say where we can and can't live even if we can afford it, much less let us take a loan to work to own something of our own. See, when we let that rage, that madness, touch us in the future and it come out in riotous righteous flames that blaze where we stay, they gon talk about us burning down our own neighborhoods, but we won't have owned none of it. It wasn't ours. It was their wealth to hold and grow like they always done."

"What they say about two wrongs?" Betty says.

"They say I'm touched. Maybe. I may be touched by God, with the traveling I do right here and the things I see and know back before when I was born and long after I'm gon be gone away from here," says Gus. He pauses for a few heartbeats before adding, "And what I done today won't hold a candle to the way folk gon take many lives out the blue, right in the middle of people's living fifty, sixty, seventy years from now. And those stories gon get twisted and twist people too. I'm tired and touched—ain't sane and might could've been done some good if I'd been sent to live at the State, at the 'Sylum, and been seen about. But here we are, Miss Betty."

Unsure of what else to say, Betty says, "Yes, here we be. Ha'mercy."

"And when it's them, these folks what call themselves white, when they bomb and shoot up our churches, it won't be them in their stories; it will be *that* man or woman. Their terrorists get to maintain their humanity and individuality—they won't reflect on the rest of them—the whole of the white folks—the *good white folks*, as we say." Gus pauses, and Betty just nods, so Gus launches in again, "That terrorist, that white, will be a disturbed outlier—took things too far—nothing they themselves would ever do. And, God help us, I'm gon be flattened into every other Negro there is—reason why they treat us so. They'll call us—paint us all as thugs and criminals—the danger, while white *individuals* will kill us at church or in grocery stores in numbers."

Betty considers what Gus has just said and says, "No offense, Gus, but I don't bit more know what you talking about than the man in the moon."

"That right there is some of what I'm talking about," Gus says. "The white man gon go to the moon in a few years. But long after that, we gon go farther. *We* gon have cities out by the stars. Those future Negroes call their homes Blackstans. Can you imagine? I been there."

"Okay, Gus, if you say so, but here we are now. I hear you, but, Lord, we here. The white folks run my daughter's husband outta town. All the way 'cross the country. That's why she live out there in California." The sand, the ocean, and the city come into the room again, but Gus isn't on the beach with Betty this time. She is in this transport by herself. She takes a few breaths on that shore and is back in the room. "He went and got on the wrong side of a white man. Stood up to him like a man, and there you have it. And still I got to go outside here shortly and tell them police something."

After a moment, Gus says, "I need to tell you, Miss Betty. They took advantage of you—sending you in here to talk to me. You know that, so I don't want you to carry no guilt behind this. I'm glad I got this time to talk to you. You know, I don't think it much matters what you tell them. Do you?"

Betty shakes her head. She knows when she exits this house and talks to officers Bolton and Murray, she will likely hear gunshots when she walks away. That's why after she says what she has to say, she heads back down the hill to her home; the cornmeal she needed from the store can wait.

March Photo Essay—Milledgeville, 1972

A throng gathering
at the Black Masonic Hall
over in Choiceville

Meet to march

Men in overalls follow a wagon
and an integrated mule team of two
—a black one and a white one—

and the rest of the marchers
follow six or seven abreast
as far as the eye can see

thread through the single arch
of the viaduct—a column
of smoke headed into town

by the campus of the college
my aunt will attend in a couple of years

Afros and right angles—
surveyed streets of a once capital
Overalls and straw hats, a bandana in a back pocket

A man in striped bell-bottoms
not to be confused with convict pants
strides behind a wagon and mules

Handwritten and hung between wagon wheels
Stop Repression in Our Town

SOUTHERN DISCOUNT COMPANY
a couple of doors up from
the white Masonic Hall
next to the Post Office
across from City Hall
and the Police Department

The stride slows to a shuffle to a gathering
in front of the seat of city government
to a stand of women and men—a forest of Afros

Hats straw and felt cocked like birds roosting
in the canopy of the standing tall crowd

Black telephone poles strung only
with wire this time rise out of the crowd

Two Afroed high school girls caught
with their hands mid-clap as if measuring
oppression—one smiles, the other's solemn

And everyone moves on
There's Sacred Heart, the church
Flannery attended right next to the Post Office

Round the corner where the GULF Station sits
with its round sign that always seems friendly
to me and there's Brookin's Market where

they hired a Black cashier not too long ago
and angered their white customers and fired
her and angered their Black customers

The sign on the side of the building reads

GROCERIES & MEATS
FRESH PRODUCE

Head down the block past GOLDSTEIN'S there
next to EVAN'S PHARMACY
Awnings over storefronts and girls with ponytails

THE UNION department store on the corner

Cars with finned tail ends
at forty-five-degree angles to the flow
of folks by the white ELKS
and the CAMPUS THEATER

back to Choiceville

Before They Could Tell Him Where to Go

They're young and newly married. They grew up in the same small town in Georgia in the middle of the last century. And he's seen a little bit of the world—Tennessee, Alabama, and framed by airplane windows: Alaska, Mt. Fuji, and the Philippines. He has Polaroids of these places that he mailed in letters to his momma, sisters, and wife while he was away—show them a very little of what he'd seen. There's been a war going on, and he enlisted to have some say in his assignment before they could draft him and tell him where to go. Having seen enough of Vietnam, he's finally back on this side of the water.

When he comes back home to Georgia on leave to visit family and pick up his wife and car for the long drive west back to Fort Lewis in Washington state, they learn quickly to wake him slowly. Though he doesn't much talk about it, he does say it wasn't as bad for him as some of his buddies. He'd kept helicopters airworthy over there. They, he and his wife, drive across the country in his '65 Chevy Chevelle SS four-speed—American muscle. They take the southern route—through Texas out to California and up the coast to Washington. They see more of America on this trip than most in their families have seen or will see in their lives.

This morning, as they check out of the motel in Flagstaff, a postcard catches his eye. He points it out to her. What looks to be an old English village with a towering bridge behind it and mountains in the distance behind that. They read the fancy script: London Bridge, Lake Havasu City, Arizona. And she wants to see it; it's only twenty miles out of the way. He wants to see it too. What's the bridge doing here? A fever dream or mirage?

A rich businessman and land developer, looking to build an oasis in the desert, bought it from the City of London—had it taken apart and carefully numbered and brought to Arizona to be put back together on a peninsula in a new manmade lake on the Colorado River. The land dug from beneath to let water flow (something to span) to create an island—a reason to cross the bridge—a destination in this landscape of sand and buttes. A gimmick? Take an old stone bridge and seed a new desert vision—this development. A bit of out-of-place past to build a future in this country to prove anything's possible.

They have dreams and will soon have a family of their own. It's 1973, and it matters but matters differently every day that they're Black and the rich businessman is white—things seem to be getting better.

The Honey Drawl

It's the summer of 2005, and I'm heading to Georgia. I've been living in the far north of the Upper Midwest for a couple of years in a place that I know many would find extreme. It's a place that can be very cold and very white. There can be subzero temperatures and a lot of snow in the winter. And also, there are a lot of white folks and not as many of anyone else. I, too, can find it extreme. I sometimes go a week or two without seeing another Black person, so it's a place where I sometimes feel conspicuous. On good days I get the sense of solitude that holds me when hiking on a trail away from cities or even at the edge of a community, as I go about my business around town. So I'm excited to get to Georgia for some sultry summer heat and, more importantly, to visit with family and just be in the first home known to me. When I board the connecting flight in Minneapolis and hear the syrup in the mouth of the chief flight attendant of the Atlanta-based crew, a blonde belle, as she greets the other passengers, I can't help but smile. That is the first taste of *home* home I've had in a while. But it quickly becomes apparent to me that she wants nothing to do with me as a passenger or a human being. She ignores me and charmingly engages the white passengers around me at the very back of the plane. With that accent, she even offers several times to bump my white seatmate up to first class so that he won't have to sit in the back. I begin to feel that she is offering him an escape from my Blackness. Once on a particularly bumpy flight, the captain came on the PA to say turbulence is like hitting rough water in a boat—nothing to worry about.

The Pull That's Sung

The cicadas' drone
like the honey drawl of home
draws me when away.

The State: An Orderly's Remembrance, 2005

with my grandmother

> In continuous operation since 1842 and at one time the world's largest mental hospital, originally called "The Georgia State Lunatic, Idiot, and Epileptic Asylum," the Central State Hospital in Milledgeville is simply called "the State" by locals and "the 'Sylum" by some who worked there.

I had to brush some of the patients' hair
and teeth. There was this doctor, the patients
liked him. 'Course, he was white. Said he was Polish.
Wasn't of this nation. Taught me the word *languid*.
He wrote it on they charts. When I got home
looked in the dictionary for the meaning.

Come to find it's got more than one meaning,
but they's all about the same, not a hair's
difference really. Come here, made a home
for hisself. Talked funny, it took patience
to understand him. This not his birth language,
but I got better at getting his Polish

accent. Wasn't no Black doctors. No, polish
shoes, cook, clean, or work fields was the means in
which most of us made a living. *Languid*,
a good word for being within a hair's
breadth of dead from tussling with them patients
like I done many days 'fore coming home.

Things had gone terrible wrong in his home
country. Come here after World War II. Polish
folks was refugees. Working with patients
at the 'Sylum showed me just how mean in
the heart folks is to those meek as a hare.
Some folks ended up there in they *languid*

states 'cause folks couldn't stand when they wasn't *languid*.
Had a working farm; growed food like at home.
Collards, corn, okra with them little hairs
that itch. Raised hogs and cows too. Made Polish
sausage. Farm was tended by help-patients, meaning
we tended the hands. Yeah, they kept patients

separated too; Black and white patients
both with fight or the same kind of languid,
heard voices or made mess the same—meaning
most of them would call a ward at the State home.
Best job in town; I could buy nail polish
and little things for my girls and keep they hair

done. Patients bought the roof that kept our hair
dry. That's a parent's meaning in life. That Polish
doctor was languid some, but always glad for a home.

The Cicadas' Drone ~ Draws Me When Away

In my hand is the small black tape recorder my father carries into the pulpit to capture his sermons. It's Walkman-sized. This is 2005. It's summer in central Georgia, and I'm visiting my parents from my new home, Bemidji, Minnesota. I'm standing in their backyard. Looking around the once large fenced area, at one time my only realm, to where the apple tree used to be, to where the fallen-down scuppernong arbor rests—so much has changed. I want to capture the sound I knew years ago and can't let loose. Holding the recorder high, a lightning rod, I hope to draw the cicadas' drone down to hold me through what'll be my third far-north winter. The drone of the cicada and the varied drawls of some of the dearest people to me, both Black and white, are the sounds that have lingered with me since leaving. The drone and the drawl both mellifluous to my heart's ear. *Drawl* from *dralen*, the Dutch word meaning "to delay" or "linger" or from the English word *draw*, which has roots in words that mean "drag" or "protract." I like to think of the drawl as extending a stay, lingering a little longer, dwelling in those words we care to put into the world. The drawl and the drone are ingrained mnemonics of the born-home I yearn for while I'm living my life away—nostalgia-triggers of a time and place when this large world felt much larger to me, when home's moorings encouraged me while setting out to follow my curiosity and explore.

Homes in the House of the Sun

At the turn of the twenty-fourth century, folks been
able to step off Earth and stride out
to Luna and Mars and plant their feet on stations,
what we Negroes call Blackstans. This time, we
determining our fate, doing what we can to keep
from being put on reservations or in the holds
of boats or in camps of detention, internment,
concentration, reeducation, or labor—plantations.
Our early 'uns mostly boarded those black-bound
boats willingly to find purpose and promise
away from the ground, to break free of the
homeworld's pull so as to build a less grave space,
to find their feet in a place without gravity and
ask each other, *What holds a world together?*

BEFORE & AFTER

Denali, 2012

Braided glacial stream, says the university chancellor's Alaska-born-and-raised wife to me on this field trip for new faculty, pointing to what I see as what New Mexicans or Texans might call an *arroyo* or a *wash*, a weave of water running in a wide and mostly dry streambed, speaking a poetry of this landscape in that image; landscapes have a shape, which is to say a form, the way my Georgia-born-and-bred father shapes language when boasting of his speed with his *I made it run like a scalded dog* to describe how fast he drove whatever vehicle wherever he was going or his *he got wind in his cheeks* when talking about a friend's blustery off-putting huff, but that is language, not landscape, which, again, has shape or form, which is not the same as syntax or order, which I suppose landscapes do have, but they're not necessarily linear like syntax, an ordering and unfolding not to be taken as a whole until walked into and understood, read, like a life— life in hindsight perceived, perhaps how some understand a lineage— the lines we stream from, which gets me to the fact that I've moved about as far north, as far from Milledgeville, as I can get and still be in these United States, and here I learn about braided glacial streams and Captain Michael A. Healy, the federal authority in the Alaska Territory in the last couple decades of the nineteenth century, who, as it turns out, was born twenty-odd miles from Milledgeville, near Clinton, in 1839 on a plantation owned by his father, Michael Morris Healy, an Irish immigrant, who also owned fifty-odd folk of African descent, including the mother of all his children. I've always known the way I am among others and my inner life flowed from my mother, whereas I've always been told I take after my father—my face and the timbre that enters the world as I shape the breaths I push past my vocal cords—and I hear it more each day; these are the stories we hold or are told to make sense of our lives in community or in the quiet times away, which I like as my mother has. Syntax is an arrangement, an order to aid understanding, and the fifth of ten children who followed the status of their mother, the eventual Captain Healy was born legally his father's chattel. My father will braid language to breathe out a poetry of the man-made world around him and the folks he holds dear when ten years hence he says *the bed will take her strength* when talking about my mother's need to get up and use her failing body, and I'll again be too far away, but today in Alaska learning how to call shapes water creates in this new-to-me landscape and finding a fellow Georgian, another man with a Black mother, who somehow found his way here comforts me in this place called The Last Frontier.

Fairbanks, Alaska, Late August

I can't convince myself the trees are sick
any longer. They yellow not because
they're ailing; it's the sun's angle and the prick

of the chill here in August by the Arctic
Circle and this day, this crossing a line, the cause.
I can't console myself as the breeze flicks

yellow leaves from trees as if to tick
off passing moments. Leaves changing gives me pause;
we're paling at the sun's angle near the Arctic.

Today the leaves turned the particular tint
of DEAD END signs I find after my wrong turns.
I can't convince myself the trees are sick.

Just now the air took on this season's peculiar scent,
and I'm sure the ravens' caws are guffaws.
Their calling and the sun's angle worry and prick

me. All the changing leaves my nerves raw and spent.
Fretting too much, like us all, one of my flaws.
I can't convince myself the trees are sick—
failing leaves and light poison me like arsenic.

Fairbanks, Alaska, Early September

All the changing leaves
me wanting to stop.
I need to balance.
Here we're in the cusp.
Time more a feeling
than a moment, less
measure than act such
as a gasp—a quick
rising of the chest,
intake of breath as
now the leaves all change
right now just here
this evening on
this trail gilded by
time—more than a feeling,
reminds me of Las
Vegas—the Golden
Nugget's dazzling
facade inviting
me to try my luck
when I maundered down
The Strip or when I'm
home visiting and
my brother and I
go for a friendly
game of pool and his
English and his leaves
leave me little to
do but lose. These leaves

the one ball's color
that he wouldn't let
me hit nor any
of the others. Such
wanting then as now
halting me with these
leaves as they whisper
and meander down
to the ground. They've
changed, and I'm less
aghast than astonished
here in the thunderclap
of this sudden fall.
I need to balance
right here on this gilt
path under these leaves.
All the changing leaves
all the leaves changing.

Musica Universalis: A Nocturne

—Fairbanks, Alaska, October

Each night this twenty-first-century frontier town settles
enough for me to hear the thrum and hiss in my ears,
my tinnitus, which I choose to think of as the harmony
of my firmament—all so far away—like the whoosh
and hiss from Nana's gas heater that warmed the winter-
chilled bedroom in Georgia while she got the skillet sizzling
with country-cured ham in the kitchen. My refrigerator
occasionally wakes this hour to clear its throat and rumble on
over the sounds in my ears. And some nights I get out
of bed to go stand under the generosity of stars here—I've
decided that must be the collective noun for all the stars
in one's gaze, the way scarcity must be for any number
of scars. There is never enough healing. Like how we refer
to a flock of starlings, a black cloud moved to billow and spill
across the sky, as a murmuration. I stand there and use my hand
to shade my eyes from the streetlights to better see the stars.
Our new light competes with the old the way the clamor
of our fleets in this age after sails is said to interfere
with the songs of pods of whales. Here I sometimes see
the aurora borealis pulse, shift, and ribbon, silent over town,
which seems impossible, like the end of the world, for we know
that light in the sky—lightning and its often not-far-off companion,
thunder—seems to say something will always follow. For centuries,
some have said the northern lights sizzle—this, I thought,
a synesthetic weaving of the senses exalting this light or
a lark like the bird we call an exaltation when in numbers
great or small—more than a handful, the way a friend

used to count lovers when we were younger, told me he was
onto the second hand. Love, while a lark, still handled carefully
in those days. And now with instruments sensitive enough,
  science says
the lights do indeed buzz, crackle, swoosh, and sizzle. I should drive
out of town with open ears to view these lights against
  the sky—black
as a raven. They often fly in pairs or groups—an unkindness,
a conspiracy, a storytelling of ravens.

Postcard from Compass Rose

I've been traveling lately
without you. Remember that
time you said I was the flower
drawn in the corners of maps
by careful cartographers to give
you guidance? A lodestar leading
you so you may not be alone—
may find your way back home.
I got word you miss me, but it
doesn't show in your ways. Now
you leave home with just your
smartphone and trust in GPS—
a guiding hand, a trying-to-be-
charming voice—and you're made
to feel comfortably lost, never
knowing where you are except
on the way, as far as I can tell.
Is that like falling in love? You
know, my face was first traced
by the winds I kissed the mouths
of, as have many men—explorers
and those who came after—
looking to see the world. Best
of luck along your way
to where you want to be.

Goodnight

with D.D.

Of snow, boulders, and trees—carte blanche.
Goodnight, dangerous, says the avalanche

to the miner as she lays down a shroud—
a clean slate to make the ruddiest miner blanch.

A miner's whisper or heart's beat, too loud.
To the pull of weight and old ways snow bows.

And the miner replies, *Goodnight, dangerous*.
Some sounds too much—the snap of a branch—

to resist at times, and she slips topsy-turvy, snow
—boulders over trees—down the slope she goes

like the flow of blood a miner can't stanch,
and they embrace under a settling cloud

of snow. When they will happen, none know.
Goodnight, dangerous, says the avalanche.

The Sight of Birds

If the sight of birds
in flight moves me
with some small joy—

If the curves of your lip
remind me not of Cupid's bow
but of the slight silhouette
of a seabird, say, gull or tern,
(the quick stroke I've drawn
in my sketches since a boy)—

If it flutters as if to keep
its place in the breeze
when you talk and hangs
effortlessly on the rising
heat of your smile—

If I can't help but watch the bird fly—

If I were a man who made
lists of such things as favorite
bird sightings, open spaces,
flat places with rises, and
distances—vistas—

If the sight of you moving
with the grace of swallows
in chase of their prey moves
me to imagine a distant place

with mountains that afford
a view of the vast and sometimes
peaceful sea and soaring shorebirds,
then I am in the place I want to be.

An Autumn Aubade

—Fairbanks, Alaska, November

We're heading toward the end, and here now
there is something missing—morning. Dawn's
not rousing till most folks in Fairbanks are
at their day jobs. Morning sleeps in here this
time of year, and who could blame it, as cold
as it is. Is it dreaming of the warm
dark of the South? In this long night that came
in what should've been the early evening
or even late afternoon most other places,
gauged by the clock's dance with the sun,
(nine-to-fivers driving in the night both ways
on weekdays) you and I have held hands, had
words and dinner, danced, tumbled, and tussled
before wrestling—my snoring, your nudging,
and the dog's budging only to snuggle closer—,
and now I need to get up and write
this poem before I return to your bed, the only
warm dark night to be known here, just before
the sky lightens to that blue that precedes
the peachy dawn so the streetlights can sleep.
This new day's sky affords enough light to see
your face and sate my need to see you again
before you wake to see me before we rise to get
about our days or, I hope, stay in bed a little longer.

Hello

She, being the midwife
and your mother's
longtime friend, said,
I see a heart; can you
see it? And on the gray
display of the ultrasound
there you were as you were,
our *nugget*, in that moment
becoming a shrimp
or a comma punctuating
the whole of my life, separating
its parts—before and after—
a shrimp in the sea
of your mother, and I couldn't
help but see the fast
beating of your heart
translated on that screen
and think and say to her,
to the room, to your mother,
to myself, *It looks like*
a twinkling star.
I imagine I'm not
the first to say that either.
Unlike the first moments
of my every day,
the new of seeing you was *the* first
—deserving of the definite article—

moment I saw a star
at once so small and so
big, so close and getting closer
every day, I pray.

What Was North

What used to be north for me was a little town in Minnesota called Bemidji. When I was a boy, a teacher taught me that north was at the top of the map, and in the world, I confused west with north as west was where the sun slept. It took me years to see things clearly. Born and raised in Milledgeville, following the sun, traveling the parallel, would have gotten me to California (to the oceanside town of Encinitas, to be exact) not to Bemidji nor Fairbanks, Alaska, the next north I would know. North is a matter of perspective.

When I was a boy, I learned (aside from the way the needle points) north was where what was once freedom to some of my ancestors could be found. Measured in degrees, north and freedom are framed by culture, weighted by history.

That teacher taught me later about the North Star and the drinking gourd or Big Dipper; I've followed it and the Alaska-Canadian Highway (a rallying wartime project to make this land safe from Japan) to Fairbanks where I found a woman—a life love—and, eventually, our son.

While we were outside of and between American borders, him in utero, wending our way through Canada to her *home* home, Carmel-by-the-Sea, a place where the folks gather on the beach each evening to watch the sun sink—cede the evening to the night—and sleep, we pondered race in America. On that road that over three thousand—not a small number—Americans of African descent had a hand in building (Black soldiers the US government wasn't sure could stand the cold, much less cut a road through wilderness) in the midst of our thinking, our little family in the Forester you, his mother, white, said, *He'll never be white enough to be white in America.* This was not an expression of desire or regret, but was rather an acknowledgment of the reality of how race was built in America. Him necessarily a Negro. Built by decisions, ours and others.

One of those decisions was made in the 1640s when race was adjudicated in the colonial court to establish mores, identities, and norms. You see, three men, indentured servants who were to eventually be freed, ran away from servitude. They were a Scotsman, a Dutchman, and a negro. Upon their capture and trial, the Dutchman and Scotsman were sentenced to four additional years of servitude. But the colonial court sentenced the negro, John Punch, to servitude for the rest of his life. This was a decision on the way to the advent and entrenchment of chattel slavery in the Virginia colony.

Another of those decisions followed the ruling in the 1656 case of Elizabeth Key, a woman whose father was a European colonist and whose mother was an enslaved African. Key's suit to have her status follow that of her father, as was the custom and law of the time, was successful. And following her success, that law was changed by the men who pen such things to *partus sequitur ventrem* (from the Latin *partus* meaning "offspring," *sequitur* for "follow," and *ventrem* meaning "belly" or "womb"), so that status would follow from an enslaved mother and not a free white father. This, a convenient law—a fairly new way of seeing the power of women without ceding power to women—served to secure power and swell wealth for white supremacy.

What used to be north was where the rare white father among the many sent his owned children begot from his owned woman out of enslavement. This is what Michael Morris Healy did for his kids. He would visit them on business trips, but they could never see their mother again.

I learned north was at the top of the map when I was a boy. What used to be north for me was Fairbanks. North is a matter of perspective. I think about those mostly southern Black men sent north into the wilderness of Alaska away from Canadian towns and villages to work south toward their white counterparts to come together at "Contact Creek" and complete the Alcan.

We made the over three-thousand-mile (not a small number) trip to Carmel in late May. We stayed through July before driving back to Fairbanks. With daily walks down to and along the beach, trips to the farmers market, evening meals with the sound of the surf coming up the hill, those months in Carmel were paradisical in my remembering.

Before our son would ride this world on a second revolution around the sun, our family would move to Georgia south of my hometown. And though Milledgeville would be north of us, and north is a matter of perspective, it would never be what was north—those norths I have called home.

Life, Yet: In Carmel

In this well-heeled California seaside tourist town,
my eyes are drawn
to the flowers that attract the Anna's
hummingbird in the bustling open-air
shopping plaza courtyard.

This is not
the parking-lot-fronted shopping center called a plaza
where I saw house sparrows
scrabble for crumbs between cars
or the skylighted air-conditioned mall atrium with its fake
flowers I know from my Southern youth.

This plaza with Mission-style chairs
and sofas with comfy-looking cushions
is ringed by three stories
of high-end shops
and isn't a town square.

I'm behind the plate glass of the café/
ramen shop where I swear I hear
the barista say to her colleague *praise*
every day.

I've looked over the menu,
glanced at the rice dishes, but I'm here
for the noodles, which I just ordered.

But that phrase, her command, which I
don't quite get, caught my attention
the way birds do—just now a Brewer's
blackbird. No one seems to notice
or let their eyes linger as mine do
on the blackbird on the chairback.

It flies to another—life not still here, and I
wonder about place, which plays a role
in identifying birds and most other things.

What lives here this time of year? What
telling mark, shape, size, or color is recognized?
How does it move? These are the kinds of questions
birders ask (as do we all) with various
consequences.

I thought I saw a varied
thrush once. But I was mistaken.

I know
what I heard, but what did the barista say?

My attention framed four syllables and
worked
to make sense from the sounds, similar to the way
a birder's spotting scope focuses on a bird's
parts—garnering details to identify
the whole.

What was her intention?
A comment on work—that "it *pays*
every day"? Or her girlfriend—"she *prays every*
day"? Or something more complicated—"time
stalks life on which it *preys every day*"
here in the café/ramen shop?

I'm attempting
to make this moment apprehensible. I
know the blackbird as a Brewer's by its
being here with its yellow eyes and glossy
black color going iridescent in the sun, nodding
toward green, purple, and blue—almost imperceptible
like the acknowledging nod I share in the streets with men
who look like me.

I
recognize the Anna's *squeechy squeee* call;
it reminds me of the sound of teeth
grinding or squeaky brakes easing
a car to a stop—a sound that always
gets my attention as it announces
an arrival, but I don't know

what it means any more than I
can be sure of what the barista said
unless I ask, which I won't.

Photographers frame some detail
with their viewfinders to make
something from the world. Aside

from this and among other reasons
I hang a camera around my neck
in contexts such as this to look,
perhaps, less threatening in my
Black body.

If I were arranging objects from
my life like a curated exhibit or
like a still life, *vanitas*, included
might be items of worldly pleasure such as
an unruled notebook (sporadically
written in), scattered negatives, postcards
from friends, photographs of family,
an MTA MetroCard repurposed
as a bookmark, a stack of flat beach stones,
a blue Duncan Butterfly yo-yo, brown
dress shoes (shoes that fit but still pinch)
that remind me of the brown
of someone's eyes,
come to think of it,
and a shiny toy six-shooter.
Or they could lay like evidence on a table or facts
laid out awaiting a decision about,
say, my murder that someone may walk
away from scot-free.

Perhaps, in the tradition of those still
lifes
called *memento mori*, there'd be a skull; this one
turned so the jagged hole the bullet punched
on the way out shows.

The hole the bullet knocked
on its way in, a neat little circle
that my pinkie can't quite fit.

It's so tidy it looks almost
natural, an expected hole, a bland
fact that might go unnoticed, and since
it's hard to face more than one side
of the head at a time, in this arrangement
it would seem appropriate to show
the final result of all that potential
energy made kinetic on its way
to stopping.

At dawn the simple fact
of a day to come
is praiseworthy, and at dusk having
witnessed
its passing holds some affirmation.

The blackbird doesn't seem to mind
the people as it goes about its business of getting by.

In the Beginning

Places to start: our mother's heart, first
sound to prove our ears—tells us we're not
one; or the fish, fowl, cattle, and thirst
for dominion and those words beat to wrought

this reality; or *one fish, two fish*,
since two is all one needs to make Other
of another, which explains our clannish
ways. Though I'm from a small town and Southern

—I know the tropics and snows and the ways
of their folks, how they make *the people* of
themselves, but of others, colors and vague
shapes as here I've done the same and struggled

not to and failed. From beat one there's no end
to the spreading differences we apprehend.

What Luck

This morning my dad called and said he was *leaving out of* my *old stomping grounds*, my beloved university town, Athens. *With twins* was his reason why; you see, in his retirement, my father works for a funeral home part-time. Transporting bodies is among the things he does now. He said they were his *second set this month* and that *we're lucky*—including himself, and I tensed as I was holding my son—only three weeks old—against his counting his luck with mine, with ours—and perhaps too soon—and was ashamed of the small moment of greed he could not see as he said, *They wasn't no size*, and I imagined them only a little larger than my two hands come together, palms up, as if begging. In that town I knew a woman who had LUCKEY tattooed across her wrist—the L where it pulses, an E dropped in, turning the second syllable to KEY—a start-of-day reminder of a coffee date with a friend whose last name was Luckey the day she got news of her biopsy—traced with needle and ink. Didn't want to forget.

Almost Solstice Serenade

—Fairbanks, Alaska, June

We're heading again toward the endless—
wait, this description hinges on a "without
-ness," a "lack of" end, when what I mean
is the longest day and hence shortest night

of the year nears, so perhaps I should say
We heading for that lasting Hallelujah Light!
which sounds apropos to a sermon in one
of those weeklong church revivals of my

Southern youth, but I feel I might ought
to be in mind of a serenade—a croon
to smooth my way into our sun-lighted
evening, an offering to you with the hope

we'll ascend the stairs soon into the needful
and loving night you created, sweetheart.

Bless those blackout curtains you hung
to turn our second story into a night away
from the well-lit surroundings outside our
walls where, when it comes, the civil twilight,

that light thrown back over the horizon
toward us, so bright we can see after sunset,
bridges the sun's leaving and greeting us.
Civil twilight sounds as if it could refer to

that nostalgic light a couple casts on one
another just before going their separate ways
or a nation of folk the sun's setting on while
they're not paying attention to the vital

things or holding the wrong things too close
to their hearts. May that be never us, my love.

One Saturday Morning in Carmel

It was spring in Carmel. There were birds. It always
feels like spring in Carmel. It still felt like deep winter
back home in Fairbanks. There were bushtits and band-tailed
pigeons, acorn woodpeckers, western scrub jays,
and a brown creeper, black phoebes, spotted and California
towhees, a Townsend's warbler, and others; a gull floated
high overhead. I stood on the patio in the least layers
I'd worn in months. I held you, legs wrapped by my right arm,
between my wrist and elbow your seat. You'd only recently begun
pointing out the living room window at trucks and cars moving
along the hardpack snow on the road back home. There were
birds—a whole new community for you—and the American
crow on the wire was the largest, and so I thought the easiest
for your young eyes to perceive, so I pointed up at it, and you
pointed with me with what was surely my hand when
I was your age, but your eyes didn't follow our fingers.
They looked to me and out and inward like when we
listened to music in the kitchen back home in Fairbanks
with our waving hands in the air, but on the patio there
was no music save birdsong. I pulled my hand back
and jabbed it at the crow, and we're doing an old disco move.
I leaned back with you in my arm and watched your eyes
roll down in your head to stay level to the horizon.
After a couple of tries the crow cawed and ruffled its feathers
at us, and you discovered it. Oh, your emphatic finger showing me
that there was a crow on the wire—acknowledging that bird
and then others. You revealed not what I knew—that there
were birds one Saturday morning in Carmel—but made me feel
again how the world opens before a curious body—our bodies.

glanced at the ***rice***:

Tamir Rice—Age 12 when killed. Killed by gunshot inflicted by an officer of the Cleveland Division of Police on November 22, 2014.

|

when rice was king / it reached the throne / on the back of / Blacks' stolen sweat / and ingenuity / rewarding the / pockets of [white] men. |

worked *to make sense*:

Monroe Nathan Work—Age 78 when he died in 1945 at home in Tuskegee. Worked as a leading sociologist and founded the Department of Records and Research at the Tuskegee Institute, which published the *Negro Year Book*, an annual record of African American life that included reports of lynchings.

garnering *details to identify the whole:*

Eric Garner—Age 43 when killed. Killed by suffocation due to an officer of the New York City Police Department administering a(n) [illegal] chokehold on July 17, 2014.

*an **MTA MetroCard***:

Henry Dumas—"An absolute genius" according to Toni Morrison, this poet and fiction writer's career was on the rise at the age of 33, when he was killed by gunshots inflicted by an officer of the New York City Transit Police on May 23, 1968.

that remind me of the ***brown***:

Michael Brown Jr.—Age 18 when killed. Killed by gunshots inflicted by an officer of the Ferguson Police Department on August 9, 2014. See also Ferguson, MO, and Ferguson Protests. See also East St. Louis "Riots" (1917). See also the US Supreme Court *Plessy v. Ferguson* ruling (1896).

someone may walk away from ***scot-free***:

Walter Scott—Age 50 when killed. Killed by a gunshot inflicted by an officer of the North Charleston Police Department as he ran *away* to evade arrest following a daytime traffic stop for a nonfunctioning brake light on April 4, 2015. Struck a total of five times.

*a **bland** fact that might go unnoticed*:

Sandra Bland—Age 28 when found dead while in police custody at the Waller County Jail, in Waller County, Texas. Found hanged in a jail cell on July 13, 2015. Bland was arrested and charged with assaulting a police officer after having a heated exchange, having been pulled over for failing to signal a lane change.

|

so much depends

|

NOTHING BUT POTENTIAL

Dangerous Goods [Redux]

In 2017, when our son was two months shy of two, we'd only been in Georgia a month. My wife and son had moved with me across the continent from interior Alaska to Statesboro, in southern Georgia, for my new job. The small university town was a couple hours south of where I was born and raised—not far from my parents and kinfolk.

It was August in southern Georgia, and I thought it would be nice to spend time with my son at our new neighborhood park. It wasn't a kids' park—no playsets, no slides, kids' swings, merry-go-rounds, monkey bars, or other climbing things. It was a green space with a big pond. An unexpected fountain sprayed up from the pond's middle. We saw a green heron at the water's edge: it took flight at our approach and alighted in a tree on the far side. There were Canada geese—thirteen of them—feeding near shore, taking turns with their heads under and bottoms bobbing up. Seven mallards—three females and four males—and a couple of feral white ducks paddled nearby.

Stationed around the pond were the type of swing that you usually find on a porch. I sat us on one. The white ducks came ashore, approaching with bold curiosity—suspecting we had food for them. We didn't. Their nearness made my son nervous. I tried to calm him with engagement. I said things like *Look at their feet*; *Their webbed feet help them to swim along the surface of the water*; and *This is why we don't feed wild animals*. I wanted him to know they could be dangerous, even as I sought to calm him so he could appreciate them.

Dangerous—able or likely to cause harm or injury, likely to cause problems or have adverse consequences—the adjectival form of "danger" from the Old French *dangier*, based on Latin *dominus*, "lord." The original sense was "jurisdiction or power," specifically "power to harm," hence the current meaning "able to do harm."

On November 13, 1995, a flock of snow geese—a little smaller and stockier than Canada geese, more duck-like—migrating south landed on a body of water in Butte, Montana, known as the Berkeley Pit. Migrating snow geese roost on lakes and wetlands. A storm may have driven them to land where they did. They died. Over three hundred bodies floated in the Berkeley Pit. There were chemical burns on their bodies, in their throats.

In that not-large Georgia town, on a family outing to the farmers market that fall, we saw almost everyone we knew and met a few new people. We walked a friend—my new colleague—to her car, and she told our son to be careful in parking lots because there is "the potential for danger." I appreciated her concern for his well-being, but I thought and said, "Danger ain't nothing *but* potential."

Good, as in material or commodity, has potential to be hazardous somehow to us when near as in "dangerous goods," things transported in boxes by truck, in cargo containers by boat, in crates by freight train, things contained, packed, shipped.

Just shy of a year in Georgia, my wife, a Westerner, got a much-desired job in Montana, so we packed up and moved again.

The Berkeley Pit was one of the world's largest open-pit mines when operations ceased on Earth Day 1982. The pumps that kept it from filling with groundwater were shut off. The water that seeped in mixed with materials exposed by the mining operation, resulting in a toxic, turquoise-colored pond. Reminds me of those stunning lakes and streams of glacial milk—colored by rock flour—I've seen in Canada.

What's in the truck? The pit? The pond? The bird? The body? The black, brown, red, yellow body? What's in the swarthy body? The Italian and the Irish body? The other body? What's in the Other's body? Let's not forget the woman's and man's body, the trans always-was-and-now-am body. What's in the bird's body?

Inside and out—the separation of this from that—*dangerous* is in placement and proximity and perception. *Dangerous* begins where? *Dangerous* meets *good* where? The *ability* to do harm *does* harm when . . . Does dangerous begin for African Americans when *20 and odd Negroes* meet the colonists of Virginia in 1619? What is the land of origin? Where is the bill of lading?

What will I tell our son? What can I tell him about his brown body? What should my wife and I tell our son about his body in proximity to danger?

You, our son, are a frontier, beyond my settled space, this life I've lived until we met between horizons. You have my teeth, or rather the gap, the space between your top two front teeth, what the dentist calls a *diastema* from the Greek for "space between," a span that they always offer to close, these white dentists, without seeming to understand it connects with family, both my mother and father inheriting it and passing it on to me. I was as happy to see that span when your teeth began to come in as when you came into this world and I counted five fingers on each of your hands and on each of those feet of yours five lovely, long toes. My aunt would call them "Papa toes" after those of her great grandfather whom I didn't know, but you, he, and I share toes.

Mixed race, you, our son, are a border—not between your mother and me—between the past and the future, between life and the power to determine one's own and set terms unfettered. Borders demarcate nations—*nations*, from the Latin for "born"—places of birth or rebirth for those who cross borders, and you were born in an old space between nations based on how lines have been drawn by the hands of men with more power than I can hope to have.

A woman of color, a colored woman, Healy's mother is sometimes called "mixed race." My sense of things is that in part the "American" part of "African American" means mixed race. Which isn't quite the same as blood quantum, that scheme, another US government imposition, meant to serve white supremacy instead of Native sovereignty, the right of self-governing for Native Americans, who before becoming that were simply *native*, meaning born here for generations to the far edges of memory, and called themselves by the names they called themselves in their own tongues.

My hand's the brown of a paper bag till I pick one up, then it's darker with red undertones. Though I've been told your hands are my hands—I knew this with a little fear—your hands are lighter than that same sack that would have kept me out of the club. Fear is an opportunity for change (depending on how it is met), for questions, for seeking answers, for a more liberated and expansive way of being in our bodies and selves.

To Be Born in the Briar Patch

Our family had been in Statesboro a little over a month and a half, and we were still learning our way around. Some of that orienting happened while driving our toddler around, so he would nap. That's how I found the local water park and recreational center my cousin Janelle had told me about when she learned I was moving here. This Sunday afternoon seemed like a good time to take our not-quite-two-year-old son across town to play and give his mom some time to herself.

We started at the playground that turned out to be for slightly older kids. It had higher slides, and there were too many kids—taller, surer on their feet, and running to prove it. This all seemed a little imposing for my son. We went to the younger kids' playground, and my son and I had a great time for a while. As I played with him, I noticed as he entered the tunnel connecting the two sections of the playset for perhaps the thirtieth time that, above and just to the right of where his curly hair brushed the top, someone had carved KKK into the plastic and apparently, someone else had carved Amen and perhaps yet another person had carved an arrow from the box carved around Amen to the KKK.

I'd applied for and come close to getting the job I was in a few years earlier. On that first interview, I was asked whether I was trying to leave Bemidji, Minnesota, the place I lived at the time. My honest answer was that I wasn't trying to leave northern Minnesota, rather, I was trying to get to southern Georgia. That was the case in the second interview as well. I had, in Alaska, great colleagues and fantastic students, Fairbanks is endlessly fascinating, and there's a very supportive artistic and literary community there. I could stare at Denali from my office window on clear days. The job in southern Georgia was "much desired" because of the colleagues and the students and the scope of the program and the department. And, perhaps most importantly, it was two short hours south of Milledgeville. I desired to get closer to home—my parents and the rest of my kinfolks. By the time I had the second interview, I'd been living outside of Georgia for seventeen years—mostly in the Upper Midwest, on the West Coast, and in Alaska. This would be a homecoming.

Central Georgia has a rich literary history. The nineteenth-century poet Sidney Lanier was from Macon; Jean Toomer's groundbreaking book, *Cane*, was inspired by his stint as a school principal in Sparta; and Flannery O'Connor called Milledgeville home. And just twenty miles north and west of Milledgeville sits Eatonton, the home of Joel Chandler Harris and Alice Walker. Of them all, it may be Harris's characters who are the most widely recognized around the world. Harris was a writer and folklorist. He collected the folktales of the African Americans enslaved on the plantation where he apprenticed as a printer's devil on a newspaper. He retold those tales years later in the newspaper he worked for, using a character he invented, Uncle Remus, to tell the tales.

KKK←Amen—I'm not sure how many hands were involved or in what order these things were scratched, but it read to me as if someone made a succinct statement endorsing white supremacy, and someone else, perhaps, seconded that notion with "amen," and, perhaps, a third person carved an arrow from Amen to KKK for clarity and emphasis. As he stood assessing the tunnel each time before entering, my son's head and hands were inches from this message/declaration/warning. I was born and raised in Georgia, and I'd brought my family here. This was our new home, and I had to think about what I would eventually tell my son about this place and how to read its signs.

At some point in my childhood, I was introduced to the Uncle Remus character Br'er Rabbit. I've heard *br'er* pronounced so that it rhymes with *care* or *fair*. I wondered at the word for a while until I came to understand it as the result of a contrived dialectal elision of the *o*, *t*, and *h* in *brother* as Joel Chandler Harris heard it and chose to represent it in his stories. I've always translated it in my head to *bruh*. Growing up in Milledgeville, that's the way I heard it come out of the mouths of folks in my community in church and on the street. I like *br'er* as a kind of shibboleth. I know the speaker is referencing Harris and not the vernacular or community I grew up with when I hear that rhyme with *fair*. And it doesn't sound too far off from *briar* as in the briar patch, the setting that plays an important role in the Tar Baby tale. Bruh Rabbit triumphs as the end of this tale by convincing Bruh Fox that throwing him in the briar patch with all of its sharp thorns would be the cruelest torture Bruh Fox could use to punish Bruh Rabbit. Surely the thorns would rip Bruh Rabbit to ribbons. But as it turns out, Bruh Rabbit was born and raised in the briar patch; it's his home. This extreme environment is where he thrives.

Before moving to Georgia with me, my wife had never been to the South—to a Southern state—except for two brief visits the previous two winter breaks to introduce her and our son to my family and friends. Wanting to prepare her for the move, I said the South would likely feel more foreign than moving to Canada. It's my home, but I think it's the part of the country that would feel most culturally and historically unique to someone not born there.

In Alaska, my wife and I had bound ourselves to each other, and she had given birth to our beautiful boy there. And in some ways, I think, that place and the community there made those actions feel possible for her. And she was game to move to the South, but she was uncertain and anxious about the reception our family would get living here.

Moving from one place to another, no matter the distance, becomes an adventure when danger enters the picture. The way one's able to face the danger—whether one can move through it or is stopped—delineates adventure from disaster or even catastrophe.

My and my son's encounter with the white supremacist graffiti visually brought home the threat to non-white folk in that environment. It complicated the briar patch. I understood and felt the threat written on that playground toy differently in the company of my son than I would have when I was growing up there, before I'd traveled away, or even when I'd return as an adult before he was in the world. Living my life had given me a sense that I'd be able to handle myself in whatever situation arose. But the failure to protect my family, my son, would be unlivable.

Bruh Rabbit convinces Bruh Fox to view the briar patch as an inhospitable, even unlivable, environment. Extremophiles are organisms—microbes—that live in what we humans consider extreme environments, like down in the deepest, darkest parts of the ocean, like the Mariana Trench, beside volcanic vents, in an unlikely lake deep under Antarctic ice, and in the scalding waters of geysers in Yellowstone. They also live in man-made extreme environments like toxic waste sites, such as the Berkeley Pit.

As a Black Southerner who's traveled and lived outside of the South, ofttimes in rural (read: overwhelmingly white) parts of the nation, I've been viewed as an extremophile. Northerners have wondered what it's like in the South and assumed I must be glad to be away from the extreme racism they imagine while being blind to the racism practiced in the North aimed at Native folk. And Black folk have wondered what it's like to live outside of the safety of a Black community in such predominantly white places as northern Minnesota, Alaska, and Montana—extreme environments for Black people.

The economic system of chattel slavery based on the invented concept of race that was imposed by English colonists upon the various African peoples that were brought to these shores is the foundation upon which America and its wealth was built. This racist structure is the origin of the extreme environment Black folk have lived in for four hundred years. And though the fact that when they constructed a race, we made a culture—something we can live in—might lead one to conclude that Black people in this country in general are extremophiles, we're not. When talking about "extremophiles" and "extreme environments" we're using relative terms based on what we humans find comfortable or simply livable. It's ridiculous and incensing that I have to write this: Black people are human, and our Black lives matter.

I am not an extremophile. Black folk are not Bruh Rabbit, and white people aren't Bruh Fox, though they understand home differently as they shelter in the power structure that is the privilege of whiteness.

But America is our home, our briar patch. Black folk were born here. And while the best of America's ideals protects us and all its citizens when realized, often in practice what happens in this briar patch cuts Black lives to ribbons.

About Danger

As a new parent, I thought about the hurricane
—Irma, an out-of-fashion name in the news
that fall—and, as it roiled nearer to landfall,
how it would impact my family. I thought
one morning—the wind still out at sea—about
Jupiter's eye, red like the hot coiled burner
on the stovetop, a storm that's been swirling
for centuries and matters not so much to our
well-being—too far away to be a bother, much
less a danger—and only beautiful if you're
a beholder of a mind to find beauty in such
things. Danger blossomed when our son's
small hand drew nearer to the red coiled eye.

ANCESTORS DREAMING

What You Studyin' On: An Environmental Statement

Sometime around 1998, I sat down with my grandmother, my mother's mother, in her living room to talk with her about her life. I did this with the intent of writing poems, because a workshop classmate thought I'd brought in one too many poems about my father and pointed out that I must have a mother or grandmothers. That was true. It seemed I'd been studying my complicated relationship with my father (typical of fathers and sons) my whole life and felt compelled to explore that further on the page. But when challenged to write about the women in my family, I realized I didn't know where to start. I'd been around them all my life, but I only knew scant details of their lives; I knew them in the role of mother or aunt or grandmother but not as people outside of those comfortable relationships with me. I'd taken them for granted. So, I sat down with my grandmother and a notepad and tape recorder.

The whole experience was oddly formal and informal. My aunt would occasionally walk in and join the interview. My grandmother told me about family members from her generation or older or about my long-gone grandfather as well as segregation and what contact she had with white people. In the cozy living room of that house her father and grandfather built, she told me about when they lived on a farm in the country and how she and her brothers attended a one-room school that was behind their little country church. She told me about how the ice spikes grew from the red Georgia clay in the cold winter months. The needle ice would be there along the side of the road in the morning when they walked to school and in the evening when they returned home. She commented on how things had changed: "We used to have cold weather back then, but we don't have no cold weather now. Think it's a warning?" With this observation and question, I imagine my grandmother, a good churchgoing Christian woman, likely had in mind God's fire that is to be the next iteration of His cleansing of the world after having made a covenant with Noah saying He would never use a deluge again.

I left Georgia for Houston, Texas, in 2000 to study creative writing. That was my first time living outside Georgia. Houston felt like an expression of human ambition laid over marshland, and I loved the insistence of nature I saw everywhere there. For instance, on campus I once saw tadpoles swimming in the tire rut of a grounds crew truck where rainwater had collected at the edge of a sidewalk. In that sprawling city it seemed any declivity that gathered water at its bottom would invite life. Three years after moving to Houston, I moved for love to a small Minnesota town at the northernmost point of the Mississippi River and fell in love with that place—called it home for more than a decade. I also spent a magical year in Madison, Wisconsin, on the isthmus between Lake Mendota and Lake Monona. And then there was the gift of two years living in Oakland, California, exploring the beaches and trails of the San Francisco Bay Area. Then there was the half a decade or so when the ever-entrancing Fairbanks, Alaska, was home. My peregrinations not over, there was a too-short time in southern Georgia, before settling into southwestern Montana.

In these places—heart homes—I found that though I have my relationship with them, that relationship was limited by what I knew of the place. There's a kind of study of a place that comes with living attentively in that place for a lifetime or at least a long while. Folks with a longer history of a place can make statements like my grandmother's *it ain't as cold as it used to be*. In those northern homes, I got *the winters aren't as long as they used to be*. In Minnesota, it was *gotta get the fish houses off the lake earlier*. The coldest I saw in Fairbanks was fifty below zero, but I was told it used to be colder.

In the warming Arctic heat waves, thawing permafrost releasing greenhouse gases, and the lack of sea are major concerns, but I've seen enough to know the global warming trend is changing things everywhere, not just in cold places.

Not too long after I moved with my family to Statesboro, Georgia, south and east (closer to the coast) of where I grew up, we heard about Hurricane Irma in the news. In a few days, we went from taking note of a storm to trying to figure out how to prepare for its landfall. I wasn't worried until I went to the Walmart in town for something unrelated to the storm and saw people buying the last of the water and other essentials—the camping aisle was bare; flashlights and gas cans were all gone. And when I decided I should probably fill up the car just in case we needed to evacuate, I found that not all the pumps at the Murphy USA filling station worked and the ones that did were pumping slowly. This was unsettling and even more so when a police officer pulled in across from me and asked if there was still gas at the station. I would have assumed he would know more about the situation than me.

Once officials ordered the evacuation of Savannah, we decided we should move farther inland too. We made our way a couple hundred miles northwest to Atlanta. When it moved inland, the storm eventually made its way there too and downed trees and caused a power outage for a while.

The next summer we moved to Montana and escaped

Georgia's heat. But the following winter brought Montana's coldest February on record. It was newsworthy and concerning to the folks around us to have a month of sustained record lows in the twenties below, but having spent a few winters in Alaska, I felt more than prepared. My perspective was skewed. It brought back fond memories of acclimatizing to the long, deep freeze up there where one day I waited in line to get my picture taken in front of the digital clock and thermometer on the University of Alaska Fairbanks campus because the temperature was lower than forty below.

The following summer in Montana was lovely until the days got hazy and, on occasion, downright smoky. There are massive wildfires in Alaska each summer, and Fairbanks could get smoky, and ash could fall from the sky like out-of-season snow, but the smoke and unhealthy air we've had in Montana the last couple fire seasons feel somehow more intense—and more worrying. As much as having an active young son who wants to ride his bike and play outside in the summer, perhaps this has to do with the fact that I've stayed put for the last couple fire seasons—no conferences, vacations, visits to family in Georgia—due to a global pandemic. At any rate, I feel more aware of "fire season" and fires across the West these days.

These days, I talk with that aunt who intermittently joined my interview with her mother at least once a week. I recently asked her about a phrase I heard and used in the Black community I grew up in in central Georgia—"I ain't studdin you." It was a dismissive phrase, something said to someone to let them know you weren't paying them or their words or actions any attention. I knew the phrase as a native speaker in that community, so it wasn't till later that it occurred to me to hear it as "I am not studying you." But in our recent conversation, my aunt steered me back to *studdin*, saying, "it's not *studying*; the word is *studdin*." She offered further clarification with "*I ain't studdin you* means *I ain't thinking about you*." I was concerned with etymology, the origin of *studdin*, but for her, that didn't matter and wasn't anything she wanted to speculate on. She grew up hearing "I ain't studdin you," and the word's life in the mouths of those around her is where its meaning comes from. Being attentive to a living language in one's life—I love that relationship with words too. And when it comes to our environment and the human impact on it, I may not be studying it, but I have been thinking about it intently for a while now.

In 2005 I took a circuitous road trip from northern Minnesota to Vancouver, British Columbia. I spent time in Glacier National Park and was shocked by historical photographs that let me see how much its namesake glaciers have receded over the years. In 2015 what was planned as a Valentine's getaway to Juneau became an occasion for my wife and I to celebrate the conception of our child. We took the city bus as far as it would get us and walked the mile and a half or so to the Mendenhall Glacier Visitor Center to see the glacier. There too were historical photographs that showed how much the glacier had receded over the years. We were aghast as we stepped onto the path of parenthood and wondered what would be our child's world.

I think a fair bit about how I walk through this world in my body—a man, Black, a wandering Southerner. But I also think about the effects all our bodies—our needs, desires, and privileges—have on our environments (the places we live) and communities (all the beings we share this gas-wrapped orb—this Earth—with). Sometimes when I walk through the automatic doors of a grocery store, I go through a series of emotions. I marvel at the amount of energy and resources that goes into producing all the fruits and vegetables in the bins, the food on the shelves, the meat in refrigerators and freezers, the paper and plastics for the packaging. And I think about all the resources and energy used to gather the bounty in this way in this place. A couple times in Fairbanks I walked into Fred Meyer, the everything store, and found the grocery shelves, refrigerators, and freezers practically bare. When I'd ask a clerk what was going on, I'd be told that the boat didn't arrive. Most of the food comes in through the port of Anchorage and must be brought about 360 miles inland to Fairbanks. Then I'd wonder how sustainable and renewable it all is and get anxious. Ninety-five percent of the food in Alaska is imported, but it wasn't always this way. For millennia, people lived on the available sustenance—what the skilled and knowledgeable could harvest from their surroundings. And in the 1950s, Alaska produced over fifty percent of the food consumed there. One of my favorite places to walk and bird in Fairbanks was Creamer's Field, a migratory waterfowl refuge that used to be Creamer's Dairy, a working dairy (largest in the Interior) operating for decades until 1966. Before it somehow made more sense to import food, the dairy produced food for cows and people as well as providing an inviting stopover for migrating birds. And I wonder what we need to know for us to live more sensibly and sustainably.

A few years ago, I was in Honolulu for a conference. I'd just arrived at my hotel room and was settling in when something caught my eye partway up a distant lush green hill. It was a rainbow smudge. I went out on the balcony to look at it, and it seemed to be getting larger. It slowly grew and arced and became a rainbow. I watched a rainbow grow out of the ground! Later as I went across town to meet friends for dinner, I was overwhelmed by the number of people and the sense that, though the place was restorative for us, our presence wasn't sustainable. We were a burden.

In my living in various states and traveling around the nation, I've been struck by the homogenizing, flattening, and disorienting effect of big box stores—bastions of consumerism. I sometimes feel lost coming out of a Best Buy or Target or Lowe's to a parking lot that looks like any other. I have to look beyond the parking lot to the horizon to see where I am. Often when I look around me at the world shaped by our modern myopic willfulness, I swing between feeling sad, anxious, resigned, pensive, sardonic, regretful, and overwhelmed. I haven't spent most of my life getting to know one place like my grandmother, and some days that is a regret I hold. But most days I try to honor the ways she and my ancestors readied me to go out into the world—live attentively and do your best to support your community—which for me now is much more expansive than she was likely ever invited to imagine for herself or her grandson. I work to maintain connection with and reverence for this world we all share. Finding surprise and admiration—wonder—in our existence and nature's insistence is a studied—and steadying—practice.

The American Pika

Ochotona princeps

Like us, pikas spend their days at the work of life.
They wake to graze and go about haying and try
to keep from being prey. Foxes, bobcats, coyotes,
eagles, hawks, weasels—so many get by eating these
rabbit kin with their big, round teddy-bear ears.
Pikas prefer when it's no warmer than 78 degrees
or so to forage for grasses and make haystack caches
for the winter they'll stay awake through, and so they
must contend with trying to stay comfortable enough
to work in this rising heat. Trying to find the perfect
spot to thermoregulate—stay comfortable—they tuck
down in the piles of rock at the base of cliffs, talus.
The pikas' talus homes sit in the rocky slopes of these
Western mountains that I also call home, charmed
as I am by their enchantment. My family's house is
a large precisely arranged pile of Victorian bricks
built in 1893 that has stayed cool, so far, these
summers since. Some folks I love feel 76 degrees
is the perfect temperature for living. At the edge
of this town are encampments of people trying
to get by. Our pile of bricks has been settling for
this last century and a quarter and so is comfy for
us, its latest residents, thus far. How do unhoused
folks settle, I mean, feel settled? The houseless, like
us all, spend their days at the work of life and trying
to keep cool in this heat, like my family under our

high ceilings, like the pika seeking the cool deeper in the talus. I wonder if we all can keep from losing our home, can keep from being the prey of those folks who make hay in this latest and perhaps last season.

A Father and Son Speak About Internal Combustion

Yes, we're driving fires,
the father answers
the boy in the back
snug in his car seat.
Fire is propelling us,
says the father thinking
of the car he's steering
toward preschool and
the cares, those ever-
increasing objects of concern
that have driven humans
from their first upright strides
till we strode off the globe
as well as of the swell
of desires—go farther faster
and live in the fashion
we've grown accustomed to—
that drives the rising heat
and megafires; the fire consumes—

The fire inside that drives us
drives the fires,
he says.

A Father and Son Speak About the Painting *A Desperate Stand* by Charles M. Russell

This happens the day after Thanksgiving. After their small Thanksgiving dinner (just the son, his mother, and father), the son and his mother found the 1950s version of *Peter Pan* with the original Broadway cast on a streaming service. When the Indians appeared, his mother had to try to explain them and the problematic caricature they presented. She found their depiction difficult to explain in the way having too much context can make simple things hard to explain to someone new to the subject.

That next morning after braving Black Friday to accompany his father to the hardware store, the son says he wants to get rainbow pancakes for breakfast. "Just us," he adds. When asked whether he didn't want to go home for his mother because he didn't want her along or just didn't want to take the time, he refuses his father's framing (to his father's delight). The son had turned four only a few weeks earlier. The son says he thinks she would enjoy sleeping in.

And after they put in their orders (the son knows what he wants and orders with confidence—"I would like rainbow pancakes, applesauce, and milk, please."), the son notices the painting hanging above their booth and asks across the table, "Are those Indians?"

The father had noticed the painting on previous outings and hoped that perhaps they wouldn't have to talk about it today. He'd thought as they were being seated that maybe he should ask for another booth. He didn't. So, he says, "Yes."

The painting's frame has a little brass plaque centered along the bottom that reads "*A Desperate Stand* by Charles M. Russell." Depicted in the center of the painting is a tight knot of men—who are not Indians—circled by their horses. Eight of the men are obviously alive. One man, sprawled on his back with a rifle close by (as if fallen from his hand) is dying or dead. And only five of their eight horses are left standing. These men at the center of the composition have taken a defensive position, firing rifles from the middle of their horse barricade. In the background there is a line of Indigenous men, Indians, on horseback, riding from right to left in a slight arc, giving the sense of a greater circle. There is muzzle flash and smoke from the centered men's rifles. The men in the background are painted in such a way as to communicate speed. They are riding at a gallop around the non-Native men in the center.

"Which ones are the Indians again?" asks the son.

"The ones in the background," says the father.

"Who's that at the bottom of the picture?" asks the son, pointing to a supine Native man in the foreground in the bottom left corner of the painting. He lies dying within feet of the circled-up men and horses.

The father says, "An Indian who has been wounded."

"Why?" the son asks. And the father begins to talk about the land and Native peoples and settlers from Europe and what a home is and those European settlers—now Americans—pushing their way across this continent.

The son interrupts and asks, "Why are they not in the center?" The son is asking about the Indians.

The father tells him that there could be a painting in which the Indians are in the center and tries to imagine it for himself and his son.

The father points out to the son the perspective of the

painting and that the white horse of one of the white men in the center of the painting with its flank to the viewer draws the eye because of contrast, and then the father notices the man who's behind the horse's hindquarters is aiming his rifle over the horse's rump right out of the painting at the viewer. And he thinks he and his son who are viewing the painting are in the arc with the Indians, closing it to complete a desperate circle.

And that's when the rainbow pancakes arrive, and the son says, "If we were in the picture, I would punch the bad guy and put him in jail."

A Father and Son Speak About Perspective

This morning on the way to preschool I pointed out the moon to him, "Do you see the moon?"

"No," he said. "Maybe I'll see it when we turn."

"Did you see it out my window yesterday or through the moonroof?"

"The roof."

I've been pointing out things like the moon to him since before he could talk. Once he knew his left from his right, I showed him how to look closely at the moon to see whether it was full and taught him how to use his hands to tell whether it was waxing or waning, coming or leaving, filling or emptying.

"Okay," I said, and slid the panel back so he could look through the roof window.

"I see it."

"You see it through your window?"

"Yes."

"We have different perspectives."

"What's perspective?"

Another time, in Georgia, as I walked with him along a live oak–canopied boulevard, I expressed my gratitude for the shade—the shadow cast by the trees' leaves. I began to explain photosynthesis—that the leaves were catching the sun to feed the trees, and the byproducts were the oxygen we breathed and the shade we were enjoying. The shade just happened to be there because of what the tree needed to do to survive. The sunny sun-catching side of the leaves was the business end of the operation, not the shaded underside as would be the case for an umbrella or parasol.

"Perspective is the position from which you observe something," I said.

"What is observing something?"

"In this case, it's to look at something. And because you're back there you see it from a different angle," I said. "You have a different perspective. The farther away people are from each other the more different their perspectives. For instance, we both see that police car there at the light, but you see it from a slightly different angle. But our perspectives are closer than that of those folks there on the other side of the intersection."

A Father and Son Speak About Distinctions

Well, that's not what we call them;
they're called uniforms, says the father
over his shoulder to the little boy in his
snug car seat. *Police officers don't wear*
costumes. This at the red light that's now
turned green—the one where they saw
the police cruiser. The father muses,
Superheroes wear costumes to set
themselves apart, and uniforms make
one a part of something—says what
you cleave to. As he drives toward
the preschool the father thinks about
the way race is sometimes read as
a uniform.
A costume, he says, *is not the same*
as a uniform.

Dear Alyce,

I wonder what it was like being born in 1917 in Anaconda, a copper-smelting town to the Drivers, Lee Pleasant and Pearl, where two creeks join to birth the Clark Fork.

You were born amid a swirl of happenings (the Great War winding down, rain going elsewhere, a pandemic waiting in the wings) and were closer to copper-colored than whites, your neighbors.

The world kept swirling as your parents raised you and six siblings on a ranch outside of town.

You went to school; you studied.

Some of your neighbors (insecure? seeking security or, rather, to secure power?) joined the KKK, studied hate, attempted to whip it up against Jews, Catholics, Blacks, and you, both Black and a devout Catholic, would be doubly despised.

You devoured your studies and went on to Montana Tech and became an X-ray technician in Butte.

You could look inside folks to see what was busted or inflamed.

Your daughter Joan would let it be known that raised in Butte she felt some kinda way, likely alone, saying her face in the morning mirror before heading to school was the last young Black face she would see all day.

I'm wondering, Alyce, what advice you'd have for us raising our son in this day in our Montana home.

The Western Tanager *or* Why Montana

Piranga ludoviciana

Are wanderings the same as migrations?
I came to Montana for love, which sometimes is
how we know our destinations.

The western tanager flies here for procreation
when the snow goes wet, puddles, runs, and takes to
far wandering. Is this the same as migration?

A life is the sum of grand and modest peregrinations.
Communities bloom at the meeting of opportunity
and ambition and can be a way to know our destinations.

A fire-engine-red head cooling to orange to
a sunny yellow body with those charcoal wings,
the male western tanager flashes conflagration

or an eastern autumn, in flight. One, familiar, greeted
me shortly after we both arrived, letting me know
our wanderings weren't the same—his, a migration.

In a stand of ponderosas where a blanket of snow lay for decades
or longer, the dendrologist says these trees moved up from what's
Mexico as that quiet water pulled back, a different migration

—moving seed by seed north, generationally migrating
to where they had been and where they could live
never asking, *How do we know our destination?*

Why Montana? One among my interrogations,
both public and private like *How big is a home?*
Are wanderings the same as migrations?
and *How do I know my destinations?*

Every Different Day the Same: A Pandemic Memoir from Montana

There was talk of being prepared to hole up. And then in our state on a Sunday evening in March, the ides, we were on the eve of the lockdown. The babysitter came over while she still could, and my wife and I went out to dinner and instead of having dessert, made one last run to the store to be sure we were ready. Folks mostly kept their distance. People here don't mind being close under a roof; it's under the sky they want their room. No preschool for two weeks. My wife, a historian, was deemed essential to the state and had to keep going into the office. With an offer accepted for the coming fall, I was already comfortably between jobs, so our son staying home with me for a couple weeks wasn't a problem. Then two more. And two more. And so on. Our son was four when preschool stopped, approaching the midpoint of his fifth year here breathing air. He knew the word *virus*. In the early days of stay-at-home we worked on numbers, letters, and simple words. We got out for hikes and bike rides. The streets always felt like Sunday morning in the South, when most folks are in the house of the Lord and/or hungover, that kind of empty. The trails up the hill felt like the after-work-getting-out—always some distanced somebodies, and if we got close, a sociable distance was measured by our dogs' leashes. Every day was the same. It felt like a long weekend. I tried to avoid the daily briefings and news from around the nation of the numbers lost to COVID-19. The snow would come and go now and again. Every day different. We enjoyed it while we could. We shared shoveling and made a miniature snow family in our front yard. Corvids—the ravens, magpies, and crows—kept us company. Spring was coming and came. The long weekend began to feel too long. Each evening, to show our support for first responders and health care workers, we went out on the porch to join the chorus of howls that erupted somewhere in the neighborhood and traveled to us and that we passed along and, so, connected to neighbors we didn't know blocks away. We heard the songs of meadowlarks and of the thronging robins, and the sandhill cranes' sonorous gargles, and the calls of the magpies and chickadees that never leave. I took stock of all of our plights and privileges. Those worried about roofs above and going without food. My cousin's job gone. My friends gone to their secluded second home. Preexisting conditions of preexisting conditions. Every same pandemic different. The weeks wore on—our son's tantrum at the closed playground. He hated the virus. In Idaho, in protest of closed playgrounds, a blue-eyed mom was arrested for violating an order set in place to *promote the general welfare* of *we the people* during this pandemic. There was a protest of her arrest at the arresting officer's home. Reminded me of twelve-year-old Tamir Rice who, almost six years prior, while playing at an Ohio playground, was shot so quickly by a cop just arriving on the scene. He was a Black boy with a toy pistol. Every same day is different. And in the eighth week, things having eased into a phased reopening, the news of another unarmed Black man, Ahmaud Arbery, young, getting outside for a jog, murdered by a white man he knew only long enough to fear mortally. Shot months earlier, in February, when some of us began to worry perhaps a little about this pandemic. Every different day the same.

Give Me a Small Ocean

Years ago, when I was living in Houston, I overheard a couple of white-appearing women in a café talking. The words that rose out of the general din, out of the flow of their conversation that struck and have stuck with me were: "They have this street over there—the Champs-Élysées; it's like the Westheimer Road of Paris." They were striking in the way that Texas patriotism was for me when I first arrived. "Don't mess with Texas" and Lone Star cans touting the beer as the "National Beer of Texas." In the early aughts, Houston to me felt like a big sprawling confluence of cultures, and it also felt segregated. Whenever I try to reach back to that memory these days, all I get is those words in a drawly twangy Texas accent in some café in the Montrose area near Westheimer Road. I moved to Houston in the fall of 2000 and lived there till late spring 2003. I'm not sure whether I heard these words in the world before the towers fell from attack or in the world after things were getting back to a kind of normal. Context matters. There was a time when patriotism drove jokes about "Freedom fries" instead of French fries, because the French weren't behind us enough when the United States launched its War on Terror. Apparently, the woman I remember hearing in that café had been traveling. I hadn't traveled much then, and I certainly hadn't been to Paris, when I overheard those words. I had heard of the famous thoroughfare—the Champs-Élysées. And I knew Westheimer Road as, surely, her friend did. But I had a hard time placing it in my imagined Paris. Perhaps helpfulness moved her to make that comparison. It didn't help me imagine the Champs-Élysées any better. Maybe she was moved by pride of place, chauvinism, if you will? *Chauvinism* after a perhaps apocryphal nineteenth-century French soldier and extreme patriot, Nicolas Chauvin. *Patriot* another word that comes to us from the French. It came to French from the Late Latin *patriota* meaning "fellow countryman," which comes from the Greek *patris* meaning something like "acting on the behalf of the father/fatherland." I wonder whether Derek Chauvin saw a fellow countryman or felt he was acting on behalf of our founding fathers and this fatherland when he knelt on George Floyd's neck.

Several years ago, while in a little coffee shop in quaint Carmel, I overheard a white-appearing guy say to a friend, "Give me a small ocean." And I thought who doesn't want a small ocean—something at once vast and graspable. To, perhaps, be able to tuck the sea in your bag to see what you can bear. In the homes of the various phases of my life, I've wanted this. I've wanted to be able to see the big picture and know I was navigating my life as best as I could. I have a fear of drowning.

A few years ago in Georgia, while lunching with a friend, a woman at a nearby table of three white-appearing women caught my ear when she said, "She woke up in such beautiful places." And I wondered who *she* was, this friend not present, and what those *places* were and how *I* could come out of dreams to one of them after laying me down to sleep in this world that is not always beautiful. Breonna Taylor did not wake up in a beautiful place.

Give me a small ocean to be as wonderstruck by as I am at those *beautiful places* in which I imagine that one woman's friend woke up in.

The Lingering

Language lingers everywhere,
especially in the South where
words from the colonial days
stay alive in places like my

mother's mouth, words like
the passed-along British *progue*
meaning "to go look about for
something, to forage." She likely

never used *forage* with a jewel
like *progue* at hand. And all she
meant was they, her younger sister
and she, went shopping and spent

much of a Saturday in the streets.
My mom never got her license, so
my aunt was always at her disposal
to drive them in her Maxima and

before that, her Corsica and before
that, the Monte Carlo she sold to me
for a dollar when I turned sixteen
because that's what family does

for family. She drove them up
and down the road to the mall
and shopping centers to look
for deals on blouses, house shoes,

house coats, clothes for sons and
nephews, food for the week, and
whatnots. I was home one recent
night in a dream looking for something

I can't now remember. I just recall
the looking and that my younger
brother helped me look. It was good
until I was struck by his being a little

older than my young son but not quite
the middle-school self he was when I
left home for college instead of his now
edging-toward-middle-age self. I told

my mother about this dream the next
morning at breakfast to see what she
might make of it, and she talked about
how the stories we tell of others mold

how we recollect them later, and as she
said this, I recalled my mom's recent
strokes of bad health leaving her bedbound
and barely able to speak. That's when I

woke heavy with past stories lingering.

Sounding a Silhouette

From the living room I see my son, five years
on in the world, in the walk-through pantry
looking for a snack, and his profile backlit

by the kitchen lights takes me back to that second
ultrasound, the first view of him from the blind
of this side of my wife's womb. The tech, she, and I

spied on him, and I was surprised to see clearly
his mouth and nose, his chin, his forehead—the shadow
he casts now in profile save for his hair, again

straight and spiky like when he was born.
In the capsule of her body, his lips moved
as if he were talking to someone or like when

I'm mulling over something to myself, my mouth
a part of that. His silhouette (a word I struggle
to spell every time like *endeavor*) at once stops me

and starts me to thinking about the old way
of capturing a likeness popular in nineteenth-century parlors
and in twentieth-century kindergarten classrooms

like the one in which I sat in 1979
in the recently desegregated South
and we, lit by the repurposed projector,

white and Black all cast shadows our teacher traced
and cut out. His profile as he forages for fruit leather
bears a new bit of self-determination, takes

me to the *Written by himself* of slave narratives,
attempts to convey the state of chattel slavery,
to capture the captivity of a people, my ancestors,

our ancestors, and their descendants—us—and I
wonder what his ancestors would make of him,
this little brown boy born to circumstances, new

and old. I wonder what he will author, what future
dreams he may hold for who may descend
from him and what they'll endeavor to do.

I think about that final shuttle, *Endeavour*,
and one of its first missions, its repair
of the Hubble Telescope, our last best for sounding

the depths of the black of space, and all the rockets
and capsules tethered to mission control
by only the cord of language that got us there.

A Father Speaks to His Son About Reckless Behavior

Son, I've seen the spoils of recklessness and come
to understand all we have are these breaths
we take to make of them what we will till our deaths.

All I desire to share with you—one way to sum
up my life.

There's so much I've wanted
to show my father—these wide Western skies
under which we might sit and share the awe
of our smallness.

These days I'm daunted
by what we've not done.

These days I'm haunted
by the future and shook by the past, which attests to some
pillaging the world—leaving mere crumbs for others—
in acts of malice or breathtaking recklessness.

I've seen the spoils of recklessness, son, and come
to know the disregard for those beneath being taunted.

We need soon to lay low our Goliaths
to honor the fact that all we have are the breaths
of our lives—

defy what collides with the sacred.

After the Apocalypse *or* Notes on, Perhaps, the Future

In the apocalypse, there won't be that pleasant waft of dryer exhaust you catch while out walking.

In the apocalypse there will be, eventually, one final window that breaks.

In the apocalypse, there will be that moment when the last of the old bridges collapses.

In the apocalypse, the last billboard raised to hawk stuff from before will fall over, collapse, or crumble, and the hawk (if there are hawks) that was perched atop it will take to the air and perhaps light again on the rubble if it offers a high enough vantage.

How will joy and happiness be situated in the apocalypse?

In this, the last catastrophe, there will be one last tick of a car's internal combustion engine as it cools down after it's been turned off.

In this, the last catastrophe, the last battery will lose its charge for the last time.

In this, the last catastrophe, the last night-light will go out and not come on again.

In the final cataclysm, will there be the smell of blooming flowers or the buzz of winged nectar sippers?

In this, the last catastrophe, the last admonishment will leave from the last mother's lips and hopefully not be her last words.

In this, the last catastrophe, the last chastisement will leave from the last father's lips and hopefully not be his last words.

In the apocalypse, there will be the last Band-Aid placed on a child's knee or wrapped around a tiny knuckle.

In the apocalypse, there will be one last embrace—not shoved, but bodies meeting each other in a needful hug.

Imagine We're Ancestors Dreaming

And suppose the seas rose; what if megafires,
I mean, what if blossoms come too early, blooming
before the last frost, so starvation's looming for

the bees looking for petals to slide between.
Suppose a hundred-year drought for our loves
and bomb cyclones and hurricanes for what's

held in a palm and most all our conveniences
—our modern balms or what we take to be
necessities, things assuming roles as central

as the heart and our beloveds as we lean away
from our relations with human and nonhuman
beings, ones that if tended could blossom. Too

early blooming drives famished bears to scavenge
alleys for trash alms before they can retire to dens
under fur and fat blankets, warm. Imagine massacres

or holding folks as property, presuming a narrow
definition of worthy relations to screen others out
—the point of who is kin drawn keen. Suppose seas

of change rose once and can again, I mean, suppose
heart and imagination—hope in our time to remedy
questions or statements as dooming as *what if*

blossoms come too early, blooming? Suppose
a hundred-year drought for our loves and balms.

IN THE HOUSE OF THE SUN

A Negro Speaks of Worlds

"I'm in a nice hotel," I said. I was talking to my grandmother, my mother's mother, on the phone, and I was sure I'd heard concern in her voice when she'd asked where I was staying. Hence the use of the word "nice." I'd just called her all the way from Africa, from Kenya's capital, Nairobi, to be exact, and she was worried. I continued trying to put her at ease with "It's a city." And finally, I said, "Imagine *Atlanta*, without all the white people." My grandmother always worried about me when I traveled. This was 2006, and by then it had been six years since I moved from Georgia. But Nairobi was as far away as I'd ever been—a third of the way around the world. And I didn't know what she was imagining. I wasn't sure what she'd learned of Africa, Kenya, or Nairobi in her then-eighty years, most of which were lived in Milledgeville—half of those during Jim Crow. The only images of Africa I knew we shared were representations from television shows like *Tarzan* and *Daktari* and ads for charities with malnourished children. So, the best way I knew to explain where I was and set her at ease was to relate it to something I knew she knew a little about—Atlanta. But a third of the way around the world might as well have been another planet to her. This was in December, and it was going to be the first Christmas I wouldn't spend in Milledgeville. And my December wasn't my grandmother's December, given that I was also one degree south of the equator and it was summer. Another planet.

I've had similar experiences with other family members and other places. After the five-day drive from Bemidji, Minnesota, to Fairbanks, Alaska, I felt like I'd driven to a remote asteroid. And that feeling grew in those first few months there. I'd arrived in mid-August, and by the time I went to Georgia for my Christmas visit, I was marveling at the sun's arcing passage overhead. I stood in my parent's backyard on the pale winter grass and raved about the sun shining down on me. This was the winter sun I'd grown up with, but now I had a new appreciation for it. My parents were concerned about my mental state, even though I was trying to explain it all to them. That I hadn't seen grass since mid-October, when the snow began to accumulate in Fairbanks that year, when the temperatures also dropped to highs in the twenties below zero. And what had gotten to me without my realizing how fully it had, was the way the sun behaved—steadily lowering its arc over the months until it was thoroughly alien.

When I moved to Bemidji in 2003, *it* felt alien. I saw bald eagles more often than I saw Black people. I'd moved there in May, and by December, I'd somehow acclimated to seeing fewer folks who looked like me or most of my kin, so when I got to Hartsfield–Jackson Atlanta International Airport, I was in some sort of shock or reverie seeing the fact of so many Black bodies. This continued for hours after I left the airport and saw Black folks doing the most ordinary things—driving cars, shopping in stores, and again just being in their bodies. But after the holidays, I returned north for love. And I fell for Bemidji in its Northwoods winter with its sun dogs, light pillars, aurora, halos, and other things I got to know.

On that trip to Kenya, I decided to make my way from Nairobi to Dar es Salaam by bus, and then on to Zanzibar by ferry. On Unguja, Zanzibar's main island, I toured a spice plantation in the town of Mangapwani. The tour included a visit to the "slave caves" that were down below the farm on a beautiful beach. We were urged to enter the shallow cave. It felt stifling away from the ocean breeze. From the dark of the cave, I looked out that horrid portal thinking about folks who'd have looked something like me and who would be taken from that cave into another world, one I can hardly imagine, into the Arabian slave trade. I left the cave with my fellow tourists, and as I'm sure so many tourists before us had, we enjoyed the water of fresh coconuts expertly hacked open by a local right in front of us. We had a half hour or so to enjoy the beach. Its warm clear water was a blue somewhere between glacial milk and my sun-bleached hooptie—my freedom as a young man. It was a stark contrast to that history I'd just stepped out of and the history I brought with me from America.

When I returned to the hostel one night, the Zanzibari guys were huddled around the TV like Americans, like the guys in my dorm back in college, and they were watching *Jerry Springer*. Things got spicy, as they were always orchestrated to on an episode of *Springer*. Jerry's guests were shouting at each other as the audience egged them on with oohs and ohs. It caught my attention so I looked on with the Zanzibari, and one looked at me and asked whether most of us Americans were like that. How do I explain America to someone whose only window is the television and foreign policies we send around the world?

On a recent trip to Georgia with my son, we visited my parents' house. It was early spring, and we spent expansive minutes in the yard under the blue sky, cotton clouds, and the barely budding trees, whose only greenery was the American mistletoe. We listened to the birdsongs and squatted down to look at a roly-poly, as I explained how I did that very thing when I was his age. Things had changed, but I took joy in that moment of finding some things to share that seemed the same.

During that same trip to Kenya, I spent a few days—including Christmas Eve and Christmas Day—in Lamu Old Town on Lamu Island. On the morning of Christmas Eve, while I was waiting for a fellow tourist at the front desk of her hotel, the young man at the desk asked me, "When did it happen in your family?" And I understood him to mean when did the African get mixed with other in my family. You see, continuously inhabited since the fourteenth century, Lamu is one of the original Swahili settlements along the Indian Ocean, and like many coastal cities and port towns, Lamu is a confluent place where for centuries cultures and people flowed together in trade. I said that I was from the American South and that I'm not sure when the miscegenation or amalgamation, to use an older word, happened, but that as far as I knew, it happened during the era of slavery and the trade. That's how I attempted to explain me and my family.

I was very recently back home sitting on my parents' porch with my father and cousins of his generation. My father was born in a shack that once stood next to where his house is now. When he was four or so, his mother—what we might call "a single mom"—left him in the care of her mother and older sister while she went off to work her way through college to better provide for him. When she came home a few years later and began her career as an educator, she had someone move the shack to what's now my father's backyard—where his koi pond sits. Once that shack was moved, they built a house with hardwood floors and porches in its old place. And my parents made their home here, next door, not long after they started their family.

In this recent moment, those reminiscing cousins were remembering their childhood with my great-grandmother—

how she loved to go fishing; how she tended a small garden, where the deck beside the koi pond now sits; how she seemed to be able to make the best meals for them with little or nothing. I was grateful to be on that porch with them just listening, trying to hold onto what they were saying, as they remembered their world.

This book is at turns an expression of things I love in this world and a working through of the things that, on a good day, in a generous moment from my relatively comfortable place, I can say perplex or befuddle me. I'm trying to puzzle through our curious and bewildering existence. And when life feels closer to the bone and my feelings are closer to the surface, I might say these things fill me with sorrowful measures or rage. Perhaps I'm trying to explain my world to my wife. Or trying to explain the world to my son, a brown boy born to circumstances, new and old—born into a very old and constantly new world. Or perhaps I'm trying to explain my world to myself. Or trying to explain my world to you, dear reader. I'm lucky to be able to make this record of my mind, heart, and time like the explorer at the campfire or in the great hall or longhouse telling tales of what's across the river or on the other side of the far mountains or in the vast desert or beyond the sea. Or, perhaps, like cousins sitting on a porch.

A Negro Speaks on Community Relations in the Twenty-Third Century

This Blackstan holds me and my sib Mel,
        with Whitey on the moon.

Us Negroes living our best destiny out in the Belt,
        and Whitey's on the moon.

We on this Blackstan, so we own this Blackstan,
        but Whitey's on the moon.

I mean, we own this Blackstan much as any can,
        while Whitey's on the moon—
most things held in common here. Common health
        ('cause Whitey's on the moon)
and common welfare—lights, water, air & erything clean
        ('cept Whitey on the moon).

Us Negroes in the wonder-filled black of the Belt,
        while Whitey's on the moon.

We made a way to thrive out here in the black,
        after Whitey went to the moon.

We threw in together with our striving to make it work;
        Negroes allow any getting out this far into our orbit;
Have some always on our lips—if we got, you got,
        and we tries to make sure there's always enough.

The Blackstans hold every Negro, me and my sib Mel,
        (with Whitey on the moon)
thir and I, and all us Negroes be doing quite well.

        And Whitey's on the moon.

Did we get out from 'round that neighborhood
        'cause Whitey's on the moon?

Nah, we dove into the black to find our new selves, and
        hmm . . . Whitey's on the moon.

Earthrise from Luna ain't the same blue, so they got the blues,
        them Lunatics, you know, Whitey on the moon.

That's why all our sympathy and grace goes
        to Whitey on the moon.

from the script of the 2156 documentary *Hammer & Drill: On Exacting a Living in the Belt*

2) **a.** The Whys—Why of the Miners	
Video	Audio
B-roll: Archival b&w footage of terrestrial miners **Text**: **Why These Spaceborn Miners**	**Narrator**: With their hammering and drilling machines, these spaceborn miners feel that they feed Earth's rapacious wants, not needs, as they extract their living from asteroids.
Miner Interview: Ashleigh Seong **Interior**: An ore-processing module away from the line	**Ashleigh Seong**: What you want to know is why we're out here? Well, we work out here for the PDs—planet dwellers, for the Under Sky Dwelling Arseholes, aka USDAs. Sometimes I call them USDA Grade A Meat collectively. You see, the meat treat us like the trimmed gristle. Think they got it all figured out—off-worlding their extraction so they can live in the world. But it's gonna take more than us out here working to make their paradise.

<u>Exterior</u>: View of a refinery space station with the traffic of craft coming and going	**<u>Narrator</u>**: These miners from many lands, nations, and languages all came together to stand landless on space stations they've taken to calling Blackstans in recognition of the black that surrounds them, their new home.
<u>Miner Interview</u>: JaMarcus Vra **<u>Interior</u>**: A dom, cramped quarters where the miners live when not mining or refining	**<u>JaMarcus Vra</u>**: Yeah, we got work songs—"Miner's Refrain" by Gillian Welch, and sometimes we sing the "Ballad of John Henry." Nah, not really, I'm just kidding, but there was a push for full automation that we had to push back against. People still necessary for the work, otherwise they might have left us out here to die. Some of our heroes are folks like Chris Smalls and Dolores Huerta, Cesar Chavez, and Gilbert Padilla. So are Bayard Rustin and Ned Ludd and a whole slew of people who valued folks forcefully. And now we learning how to live sustainably on our Blackstans.

2) **b.** The Whys—Why of the Negroes	
B-roll: Archival—the blue marble view of Earth and Luna and Mars and early spacefarers going about their business surrounded by the black of space **Text**: **Why These Space-born Negroes**	**Narrator**: Some think they have embraced living in the black of space to the point of calling themselves Negroes.
Miner Interview: Ashleigh Seong **Interior**: A dom, where the miners live	**Ashleigh Seong**: Obama-ites? 'Cause we call ourselves Negroes? Well, sure, we recognize Obama signing the Space Act of 2015. But, nah. I mean, there are a few among us who speak of that political dynasty with something like reverence. That's a bit of nostalgia for what they didn't know 'cause we don't talk politics. We speak policy 'cause we all in the same party, though we might disagree. Yeah, policies, not agendas; things we need to do to get by out here and hopefully a little more.

Archival Stills: Eighteenth- and nineteenth-century etchings of slave auctions and runaway slave subscriptions	**Narrator**: When individuals gather into a community, the question of what makes them a people inevitably arises. The one-drop rule created an aggressive racial line, profitable to its inventors, during the era of slavery in the United States and made those first Negroes into the Other. Similarly, in those same United States, blood quantum was invented to get land out of Indigenous hands. And elsewhere in the then New and Old Worlds, race and caste were constructed around labor and color and blood. So, in addition to their black context, considering the ways the corporations treated them (old notions drove new abuses, no crosses burned nor nooses hung, but bulldozing all the same) for these miners to proclaim themselves Negroes seems as good a way as any to make a people. As good an identity to understand common welfare as any.

Miner Interview: JaMarcus Vra **Interior**: A dom, where the miners live	**JaMarcus Vra**: Yeah, the first folk in the Belt, that generation that didn't know they were the first—thought they would work to support life on an Earth they and theirs would return to. They grew to resent the folks on the planet who didn't expect them back and took their work for granted—those who viewed them and their generations as less than.
Observational: A dom, where the miners live	**Narrator**: Black is the color one gets by mixing all the hues and pigments together. And we are all the same color in the dark. We are all simply voices in the black. And given that, folks born in the black womb of space, from the green seed of Earth, proclaiming themselves Negroes seems fitting. This is the explanation of all the previous races, peoples from various places, all shades and slants and cants together—so many nodes of culture reconciled to one myth—manifesting the Negro nation in space.

Miner Interview: Ashleigh Seong **Interior**: A dom, where the miners live	**Ashleigh Seong**: The first and second generations born in the Belt mined those planetesimals (the dust and crumbs of the sun's house) for Earth, like a colony across the black. Eventually they got new notions of themselves, of the community they could be beyond a colony.

What You Want to Know

Look here, lean in, listen, I'll tell of our urlings.
OSIRIS–REx is our progenitor, but we come
from a long line, a race of folk who made
things. It's 2407 and folk ain't yet made
the jump to other galaxies or clusters or even
got outside our star's realm; we've no FTL
drives, but, by the Well of Grace, we have
stretched out a little in the house of our sun.
We been populating—terraforming—planets
and moons; we been mining asteroids and such.
Is this drive what keeps us in the line of humankind?

Those who came before us learned to gather
what they wanted from the ground, dig in
the earth for ore to heat and make malleable,
to shape the hard things of life that became
necessities, and so do we; as those who came
before us took to the seas in their ships to hunt
and harvest leviathans for things that became
necessities like the light from lit whale oil,
so do we in our ships in the black expanse.
At home in the black, we Negroes track
the leviathans, mining the asteroids of the Belt
between Jupiter and Mars to extract what we need.

OSIRIS-REx was our begetter and Bennu
was our beginning, first leviathan visited.

Complected Boundaries, 2338

Our culture-keepers—tale-spinners, griots, kathakars—and our primers tell us about the Amalgamation of Nations on that first Blackstan, an earlier iteration of the folks before they came to be the many siblings, before they all became the Negroes—us out on these Blackstans. They also tell of how in the United States in the eighteenth and nineteenth centuries folks and powers would talk about human admixtures as "amalgamations." As if a human can be an admixture, and as if every human ain't. Be that what it may, to us miners and our metallurgist cousins, an amalgamation was a way to make something useful of a two. We've been raised in a place where the range of expressions of Negro bodily forms the Blackstans birthed over the centuries is us—family, friends, community that ranged from noses narrow as the galaxy to wide as the horizon, not to mention the range of lips and hips and everything else including skin so light it's dang near baby's first toothed-grin bright to skin dark as you can imagine, what I mean is kin darker than tomorrow to kin brighter than tomorrow—is people. Society has taught us how to see family, how to recognize cousins and community.

There was a time when skin complexion erected boundaries, time since passed, a few generations back, skin complected boundaries. This is what we learned in squayla—when the skins on the world complected boundaries and skins elected boundaries, and minds selected boundaries there were narratives that excluded complicated histories some couldn't agree on—who done what to whom and when—when it was advantageous.

Getting through it to a more inclusive story didn't come immediately after getting through the exosphere, Earth's last layer of skin, became old hat or even when it became necessary, after The Ruin drove everyone who could leave from Earth. We Negroes here mining the Belt came to seeing all as worthy kin, cousins. Some didn't get it, living on Earth's moon—Luna. They cleaved to the old ways, these Lunatics, and called themselves White and made Luna a Whitopia. And that's why we used to say "Whitey's on the moon."

But that was a time in our past when skin complexion erected boundaries, but now there are Negroes on the moon. We Negroes keep a close eye on our security, and work to guard against it going too far, so that it don't dehumanize, vilify, or demonize any other. Our graceminders remind us not to go beyond our Negroness. They remind us to always return to the Well of Grace. We've reconciled with our cousins on Luna and our Martian cousins too. We left the ball we shared, and now we share the heliosphere—our bubble. We all Negroes in the black. We out here proguing the cosmos and negro-engineering our lives.

A Negro Speaks of Lewis Temple in 2293

You see, with his forge, hammer, and anvil—
all old-fashioned—Lewis Temple worked metal
with fire and muscle and built a better way
to grapple with leviathans in those
nineteenth-century seas. He was of a nation
of united states, and was born in a time
when the old negroes could be, and most were,
if you can imagine it, held as property
legally. You see, some of our urlings
were held and others had a holt of, I mean,
all our urlings were earthlings, but not every
earthling was our urling. Lewis Temple was
one of those negroes we count amongst
our ancestors, because what is space without
spanning, without grappling with distance?
For a span he did as well for himself
and his family as any negro could hope.
We praise Lewis Temple, a blacksmith,
an inventor and innovator, a maker of ways
for other negroes. What is space without
reaching? What is now without them, them
who back when dreamed or strived or simply
survived and gave rise to what they did not know,
us descended.

The Negroes Send Their Love

The Negroes mend their love and are : the Negroes rend their love and find : the Negroes rescind their love and lose : the Negroes lend their love and win : the Negroes penned their love but : the Negroes tend their love yet : the Negroes defend their love for : the Negroes wend their love in : the Negroes contend their love is : the Negroes end their love of : the Negroes spend their love

The Negroes mend your love : the Negroes rend your love : the Negroes rescind your love : the Negroes lend your love : the Negroes penned your love : the Negroes tend your love : the Negroes defend your love : the Negroes wend your love : the Negroes ain't niggers in space : ain't no niggers in space : we all niggas in space : when we Negroes at the table, niggas be winning at spades : the Negroes contend your love : the Negroes spend your love

The Negroes mend your shove : the Negroes rend your shove : the Negroes rescind your shove : the Negroes lend your shove : the Negroes penned your shove : the Negroes tend your shove : the Negroes defend your shove : the Negroes wend your shove : the Negroes contend your shove : the Negroes ain't studdin your shove : the Negroes spend your shove : the Negroes end your shove

The Negroes in their love : their rage, their sorrow, their nostalgia, their joy, and

We Negroes send our love : our children; we send our children into the future, into the world.

AN EPILOGUE

The Negroes Send Their Love

Many days these last few years, I'm driving through a landscape that reminds me of some of my father's beloved "shoot-'em-ups"—the Westerns I grew up watching with him (when was the Wild West?) —and thinking about distance, the span of time.

These days, I'm in a group text with my cousins, and we are sending our love. And I think about the span, the distance we are from each other. Most of the cousins are in Georgia, so their days start a couple of hours ahead of mine—their time different. They often start the day by sharing birthday announcements, which we chime into. There are a lot of cousins across the generations. And I think that any given dawn the simple fact of waking to the potential of a day to come is praiseworthy.

There are announcements of accomplishments according to the season of the year or life: success at the cheer team tournament, the swim meet, the football game, the teens completing the Bicycle Ride Across Georgia (BRAG), the speech at school or church, graduations, passing the bar, investiture of judgeship, our son's first run of the ski season, and so on. And at dusk, at day's end, having witnessed that passing holds some affirmation—I've lived another day. And, on a good day, that may hold joy.

I was called home recently because my mama was in the hospital, and the doctors had done what they could. A week later as I entered the church with the funeral procession, I saw a cousin I don't think I had seen in six or seven years. Seeing his face, I stepped out of the procession to hug him as tight as

I could. His being there that moment, his presence was what I didn't know I needed just then. The week between mom's passing and the funeral, folks from the community, classmates, and friends had been visiting my father and us with condolences and food to pay their respects. The community held us.

And after the funeral, and the graveside service, and the repast, my father, brother, and I went back to the house. A couple of our father's friends came to visit with him, and our cousins came to hang out in the front yard and driveway with my brother and me. As we sat, listening to music and sipping brown liquor, they shared stories of my mom's love for them with us, her sons.

Their stories reminded me of C. P. Cavafy's poem "Myris: Alexandria, A.D. 340," a poem I often think about when someone dies. In the poem, Cavafy creates the scene of the early Christian funereal ceremony of the eponymous Myris in his family's home. The speaker of the poem is a pagan friend who considered himself close to Myris; perhaps they were lovers. He stands at the edge of the ceremony and now finds himself questioning how well he knew his friend as he reevaluates instances when Myris's religion kept him just a bit apart from their gang's pagan revelries. The immediacy of this remembering, this drama, is moving. In the end, the onlooking outsider mourning his friend's death flees the scene to keep from remembering more and to preserve his precious memories of Myris as he knew him. In this poem, Cavafy treats the power that memory holds for us and the idea of the truth of memories and how our various relationships hold all of who we are. By having the speaker's sense of memory, truth, and shared stories waver, Cavafy presents a profound portrayal of the nature of all three, the interplay of which is how we may get at complicated truths.

In this case though, their love—my cousins' relationships with my mama—helped me to see her more fully. My cousins, they held me and my brother with their love and those memories and their listening that day in a way I couldn't have known I would need. I'm grateful for their stories and their beings that help me every day as I try to span the gulf of losing her.

Notes on the Work

7 **Necessarily a Negro** A note on notes: "*Necessarily a Negro*" started out as two of six footnotes for "Governor's Mansion Hands." These were explanatory notes, some prose and some verse, that were the speaker's necessary digressions and elaborations—part of the speaker's emotional and intellectual context in the background of the poem's unfolding. They enabled me, the poet, to begin penning the poem. And they insisted on being shared—read/heard.

When I recorded the poem for the Academy of American Poets' Poem-a-Day series, the question of how to read them arose. I tried reading the poem with the notes interpolated into its flow, and I read the poem followed by the notes. I decided to use the latter recording.

And when working on the manuscript of *The Negroes Send Their Love*, I needed to decide how to present the notes. Would they be on the facing page or on the next verso page or in endnotes at the end of the section? I, ultimately, decided to cut them loose from the poem to reenvision how they could be in conversation with "Governor's Mansion Hands." They drifted into the manuscript finding places to float, their italicized titles signaling their connection to the original piece. This was done for three poems and their respective notes in the collection.

7 ***of those negroes*** A note on *Negro/negro*: Across this book, *negro* is lowercase when used to refer to a Black person before the end of the Civil War—think before April 9,

1865, with Robert E. Lee signing the articles of surrender or, perhaps, before November 6, 1865, with the surrender of the *CSS Shenandoah* in Liverpool, England. Endings are sometimes less definitive than we think. *Negro* is spelled with a capital *N* when used to refer to a Black person after the Civil War, with the intent that the distinction represents a people's different and evolving legal status or state of being in this nation.

194 ***Whitey on the moon*** A note on new notions: "A Negro Speaks on Community Relations in the Twenty-Third Century" is a new notion that wouldn't exist without Gil Scott-Heron and his poem "Whitey on the Moon" and Tim Seibles and the po-jacking invitation he offered at a Cave Canem workshop in 1999. As one of the epigraphs for this book, Octavia Butler's "There's nothing new / under the sun, / but there are new suns" builds off Ecclesiastes 1:9 and turns it; the imagining in "Life, Yet: A Family Story" could not have happened without Butler's *Kindred*. The poem "Mary Turner's Child's Peace Unborn" owes a debt to a couple poems by Honorée Fanonne Jeffers, "dirty south moon" and "Singing Counter." I am grateful to them and to Diana Di Stefano, Deon Hill, Donald Hill, Mary Hill, Louise Mapp, Eva Mapp, Scott Ferrenberg, Caitlin Thompson, William Carlos Williams, and Corinna Zeltsman, whose words inspired me and appear in some of these pieces.

Acknowledgments

Grateful acknowledgment is made to the editors of the publications in which the following pieces, some in alternate versions, appeared:

The Academy of American Poets' *Poem-a-Day*, "Governor's Mansion Hands," "Hello," and "The Whiteheaded Woodpecker"
Alaska Quarterly Review, "Musica Universalis in Fairbanks"
The Arkansas International, "Goodnight"
Colorado Review, "November, Fairbanks, Alaska: An Aubade," "The Sight of Birds," and "The State: An Orderly's Remembrance"
Copper Nickel, "Early September, Fairbanks, Alaska"
High Country News, "Pearl & Lee"
New England Review, "They Drove: A Story"
Orion Magazine, "One Saturday Morning"
Outdoor Retailer, "Dangerous Goods [Redux]"
Oxford American, "In the Kitchen with Celia"
Phi Kappa Phi Forum, "A Father Speaks to His Son About Reckless Behavior"
Ploughshares, "Mansions Ars Poetica 1863"
Plume Poetry, "Late August, Fairbanks, Alaska"
Poetry Northwest, "Every Different Day the Same: A Pandemic Memoir from Montana" and "What Luck"
Santa Clara Review, "A Father Speaks with His Son About Internal Combustion" and "The Pull That's Sung"
Sugar House Review, "Postcard from Compass Rose"
Voluble channel of *Los Angeles Review of Books*, "In the Beginning"

Water~Stone Review, "A Father and Son Speak About the Painting *A Desperate Stand* by Charles M. Russell" and "To Be Born in the Briar Patch"

For inviting me to contribute to their projects, grateful acknowledgment is made to the editors and curators of the anthologies and exhibitions in which the following pieces, some in alternate versions, appeared:

Cascadia Field Guide: Art, Ecology, Poetry, edited by Elizabeth Bradfield, CMarie Fuhrman, and Derek Sheffield, Mountaineers Books: "The White-headed Woodpecker"

Creature Needs: Writers Respond to the Science of Animal Conservation, edited by Christopher Kondrich, Lucy Spelman, and Susan Tacent, University of Minnesota Press: "American Pika"

Dawn Songs: A Birdwatcher's Field Guide to the Poetics of Migration, edited by J. Drew Lanham and Jamie K. Reaser, Talking Waters Press: "The Western Tanager *or* Why Montana"

A Literary Field Guide to Southern Appalachia, edited by Rose McLarney, Laura-Gray Street, and L. L. Gaddy, University of Georgia Press: "Lake Sturgeon"

Solastalgia: An Anthology of Emotion in a Disappearing World, edited by Paul Bogard, UVA Press: "What You Studyin' On: An Environmental Statement"

Still Life with Poem, edited by Jehanne Dubrow and Lindsay Lusby, Literary House Press: "Life, Yet: In Carmel"

"What Was North" was featured in *Mapping North: A Visual Art & Literary Exhibit*, curated by Jil Evans and G.E. Patterson, Form and Content Gallery, Fall 2017.

"Imagine We're Ancestors Dreaming" was commissioned by the Natural Resources Defense Council (NRDC) and published on their website alongside poems by Rachel Eliza Griffiths and Jane Wong as part of a Spring 2023 special poetry feature, Poets Imagine a Different Climate Narrative: https://www.nrdc.org/stories/poets-imagine-different-climate-narrative.

For believing in the manuscript and for their roles in bringing this book into the world, I am grateful to Daniel Slager, Mary Austin Speaker, Lauren Langston Klein, and the rest of the Milkweed Editions staff.

For their support, which allowed me to write some of these poems, I am grateful to the Cave Canem Foundation, the Hambidge Center for the Creative Arts & Sciences, the Vermont Studio Center, the National Endowment for the Arts, the University of Alaska Fairbanks, Georgia Southern University, Georgia College & State University, the University of Georgia's Hargrett Special Collection, Lubrecht Experimental Forest at UM, and the University of Montana.

I want to thank Donald, Mary, and Deon Hill, and the rest of my family—my aunts, uncle, great-aunt, and the cousins—for their love and support.

And for their support, encouragement, and friendship I want to thank Adrian and the Bailey family, Travis and the Barman family, Jericho Brown, Derick Burleson, Allen Gee, Joni Tevis, Nicky Beer, Wayne Miller, Danielle Evans, Laleh Khadivi, Mathew Hawthorne, Sara Dennison, Gerri Brightwell, Daryl Farmer, Terry Reilly, Desiree Simons, Sarah Stanley, Erin Hollowell, Don Rearden, Christina Olson, Jared Yates Sexton, Robert Stubblefield, Debra Magpie Earling,

Brian Blanchfield, J. Drew Lanham, Keith Baitsell, Michael Fisher, and Kevin Young.

And for their friendship, encouragement, support, and most of all for reading this book in manuscript, I want to offer special thanks to Elizabeth Bradfield, Tracy Butts, Jeanne Clark, Diana Di Stefano, Camille Dungy, Renata Golden, Latria Graham, Pablo Peschiera, and Sheree Thomas.

And I want to thank Broc Rossell for his keen editorial eye, which made this a better book.

And finally and most importantly, for creating this life with me, I am grateful to Diana Di Stefano and Henry Hill.

Sean Hill is the author of *Dangerous Goods*, awarded the Minnesota Book Award in Poetry, and *Blood Ties & Brown Liquor*, named one of the Ten Books All Georgians Should Read by the Georgia Center for the Book. He has received numerous awards and fellowships, including a Stegner Fellowship from Stanford University and a Creative Writing Fellowship from the National Endowment for the Arts. His poems and essays have appeared in *Callaloo*, *Harvard Review*, *Orion*, *Oxford American*, *Tin House*, and in dozens of anthologies, including *Black Nature* and *Villanelles*. Hill has served as the director of the Minnesota Northwoods Writers Conference at Bemidji State University since 2012. He is a consulting editor at Broadsided Press and has taught at several universities. Hill lives with his family in southwest Montana and is an associate professor in the Creative Writing Program at the University of Montana.

Founded as a nonprofit organization in 1980, Milkweed Editions is an independent publisher. Our mission is to identify, nurture, and publish transformative literature, and build an engaged community around it.

We are based in Bde Óta Othúŋwe (Minneapolis) in Mní Sota Makhóčhe (Minnesota), the traditional homeland of the Dakhóta and Anishinaabe (Ojibwe) people and current home to many thousands of Dakhóta, Ojibwe, and other Indigenous people, including four federally recognized Dakhóta nations and seven federally recognized Ojibwe nations.

We believe all flourishing is mutual, and we envision a future in which all can thrive. Realizing such a vision requires reflection on historical legacies and engagement with current realities. We humbly encourage readers to do the same.

milkweed.org

Milkweed Editions, an independent nonprofit literary publisher, gratefully acknowledges sustaining support from our board of directors, the McKnight Foundation, the National Endowment for the Arts, and many generous contributions from foundations, corporations, and thousands of individuals—our readers. This activity is made possible by the voters of Minnesota through a Minnesota State Arts Board Operating Support grant, thanks to a legislative appropriation from the Arts and Cultural Heritage Fund.

Interior design by Alex Guerra
Typeset in Bembo

Bembo was created in the 1920s under the direction of printing historian Stanley Morison for the Monotype Corporation. Bembo is based upon the 1495 design cut by Francesco Griffo for Aldus Manutius, and named after the first book to use the typeface, a small book called De Aetna, by the Italian poet and cleric Pietro Bembo.

Milkweed Editions is committed to ecological stewardship. We strive to align our operations accordingly and to reduce their environmental impact. We are a member of the Green Press Initiative, a nonprofit coalition of publishers, manufacturers, and authors working to protect the world's endangered forests and conserve natural resources. *The Negroes Send Their Love* was printed on acid-free 100% postconsumer-waste paper by Friesens Corporation.